Contents

GET HIGH PUDDING

Preparation Time: 15 minutes - **Cooking Time:** 2 hrs. - **Servings:** 2

INGREDIENTS:

- 2cups dried figs soaked in 1/4 cup boiling water
- 1 cup of cannabis milk
- 1 1/2 cups all-purpose flour sifted
- 1 cup of sugar
- 2 1/2 teaspoons baking powder
- 1 tsp. pumpkin pie spice
- 1 teaspoon of sea salt
- 3 eggs
- 1/2 cup melted cannabis butter
- 1 1/2 cups breadcrumbs
- 1 tablespoon grated orange peel

DIRECTIONS:

1. Mix all ingredients until well blended. Pour into a greased bundt pan. Place into a water bath. Cover with nonstick foil loosely. Bake it until pudding is set and begins to release from the sides of the pan, about 2 hrs.

Nutrition: Calories: 250, Fat: 4,7g, Fiber: 1.4g, Carbs: 49g, Protein: 0.9g

MARIJUANA CREAMY CUSTARD

Preparation Time: 15 minutes - **Cooking Time:** 15-20 minutes - **Servings:** 2

INGREDIENTS:

- 1 spoon vanilla extract
- 3 eggs
- 0.3 to 0.5 marijuana flowers
- 600 grams of milk
- 90-130 grams of sugar

DIRECTIONS:

1. In a medium-sized bowl, combine the eggs and milk Add vanilla extract, dried buds and sugar Beat everything at medium speed Once the liquid has formed, continue mixing the batter for an extra two minutes Transfer the contents into a container and then let it set in the fridge Dust with cinnamon or top

with fruits.

Nutrition: Calories: 208, Fat: 1.4, Fiber: 1.9g, Carbs: 35g, Protein: 0.2g

"BAKED" PEACH PIE

Preparation Time: 15-20 minutes **- Cooking Time:** 50-60 minutes **- Servings:** 6-8

INGREDIENTS:

- ½ cup plus 2 tablespoons canna sugar
- ¼ cup packed brown sugar
- 5 cups fresh peaches peeled and sliced (see Note)
- 1 prepared pie shell or Canna Pie Crust
- 3 tablespoons potato starch or cornstarch
- 1 teaspoon cinnamon, divided
- ½ teaspoon ground cloves
- ¼ teaspoons salt
- 1 tablespoon cannabutter
- 2 teaspoons lemon juice
- 3 tablespoons heavy cream
- Canna Pie Crust:
- 3 cups all-purpose flour
- 14 tablespoons cold butter, cubed
- 2 tablespoons granulated sugar
- 2 tablespoons cannabutter, cold
- 1½ teaspoons salt
- ½ cup plus 2 teaspoons ice-cold water

DIRECTIONS:

1. Preheat the oven to 400°F. In a large bowl, combine ½ cup of the CBD sugar and the brown sugar, add the peaches, and toss to coat. Cover and let stand for 1 hour. Roll out half of the chilled pie dough and lay it in the bottom of a 9-inch pie pan. Trim the edges, leaving about ½ inch of crust overhang. Drain the peaches, reserving the juice. In a small saucepan, combine the potato starch, ½ teaspoon of the cinnamon, the cloves, and CBD salt, and slowly add in the reserved peach juice and stir. Put the pan over medium heat, and bring to a boil. Cook for 2 minutes or until thickened. Remove it from the heat and stir in the CBD butter and lemon juice. Pour the mixture over the peaches, carefully fold in, and then pour the filling into the crust. Roll out the remaining pastry and make a lattice or your favorite top crust. Trim, seal, and flute the edges. Mix together the remaining ½ teaspoon of cinnamon and 2 tablespoons CBD sugar. Brush the top of the uncooked pie crust with the cream and sprinkle with the cinnamon-

sugar mixture. Cover the edges with foil, so they don't bake too quickly, and bake for 50 to 60 minutes, or until the filling is bubbly and the crust is golden.

2. Canna Pie Crust:

3. Mix together all the ingredients except water in the food processor. Pulse 4 to 5 times, then add the water, processing just until the dough comes together—you still want to see pea-size pieces of butter. Divide the dough into two equal pieces, wrap in plastic, and refrigerate for at least 1 hour or until ready to use.

Nutrition: Calories: 289, Fat: 8.9g, Fiber: 2.8g, Carbs: 52.1, Protein: 0.9g

FRESH GLAZED VERY RED BERRY PIE

Preparation Time: 1 hr. **- Cooking Time:** 10-15 minutes **- Servings:** 3-4

INGREDIENTS:

- ½ cup regular sugar
- ½ cup canna sugar
- 1 pkg. Jell-O Raspberry Jelly Powder
- 2 tablespoon corn starch
- 1 cup of water
- 1 baked (9-inch) pie shell, cooled
- 3 cups fresh strawberries, hulled
- 2 cups fresh raspberries
- 1 cup heavy cream, whipped

DIRECTIONS:

1. Mix sugar, dry jelly powder and corn starch in a medium saucepan. Gradually Blend in water. Then let it boil under medium-high heat while whisking continuously. Cook and stir until thickened. Let cool 10 min. Fill pie shell with berries; cover with jelly glaze. Refrigerate 1 hour. Top with whipped cream before serving.

Nutrition: Calories: 265, Fat: 5.4g, Fiber: 1.4g, Carbs: 67.1g, Protein: 1.2g

BLUEBERRY-PEACH COBBLER

Preparation Time: 20 minutes **- Cooking Time:** 45-50 minutes **- Servings:** 8

INGREDIENTS:

- ¼ cup (4 tablespoons/½ stick) unsalted butter, melted, plus more for the pan
- 4 cups sliced peeled peaches
- pint blueberries (about 4 cups)

- 1 tablespoon cornstarch
- 1 teaspoon ground cinnamon
- ½ teaspoon ground ginger
- ¾ cup granulated sugar
- 2 tablespoons plus 2 teaspoons Canna sugar
- 1 cup all-purpose flour
- 2 teaspoons baking powder
- ⅛ teaspoon freshly grated nutmeg
- ⅛ teaspoon salt
- 1 cup whole milk Whipped cream, vanilla ice cream, or crème fraîche, for serving

DIRECTIONS:

1. Preheat the oven to 350°F. Lightly butter a 3-quart baking dish. In a bowl, mix together the melted butter, peaches, blueberries, cornstarch, cinnamon, ginger, and ¼ cup of the granulated sugar. Ina medium bowl, whisk together the remaining½ cup granulated sugar, canna sugar, flour, baking powder, nutmeg, and salt. Slowly whisk in the milk. Pour the batter into the prepared baking dish and top with the fruit mixture. Next, bake it until it is golden in color the filling is bubbling and thick around the edges, maybe around 45 minutes, serve hot from the oven topped with whipped cream, vanilla ice cream, or crème fraîche. Cover and refrigerate any leftover cobbler for up to 4 days.

Nutrition: Calories: 255, Fat: 6g, Fiber: 2.4g, Carbs: 50.1, Protein: 0.4g

CHOCOLATE CITRUS TORTE

Preparation Time: 15 minutes plus cooling time - **Cooking Time:** 10-15 minutes - **Servings:** 4-6

INGREDIENTS:

- 1 canna pie crust
- 8 ounces dark chocolate, chopped fine
- 6 tablespoons butter, unsalted, cut in a piece
- 1 Canna Spicy Jelly Spice Blend
- 2 tablespoons orange zest
- 2 tablespoons grapefruit zest
- ¼ cup boiling water
- 1 egg yolk
- Whipped Cream for topping

DIRECTIONS:

1. Over a double boiler, melt on low chocolate, butter, orange zest, grapefruit zest. Then, Whisk for 3 minutes in a double boiler over low heat. Strain out the egg yolk and mix well with chocolate. Pour into

cooled crust and chill. Top with Whip Cream.

Nutrition: Calories: 245, Fat: 4.1g, Fiber: 3.4g, Carbs: 49.1, Protein: 0.10g

LEMON RASPBERRY SCONES

Preparation Time: 35-40 minutes **- Cooking Time:** 15-20 minutes **- Servings:** 8-10

INGREDIENTS:

- Scones
- 2-3 cups cake flour
- 2 tsp. baking powder
- 1/4 cup sugar
- 1/2 teaspoon ground cardamom
- 1 tablespoon lemon zest (zest of 1 lemon)
- 5 tablespoons cold canna-butter, cut into chunks
- 1 cup heavy cream, plus more for brushing before baking
- 1 cup frozen raspberry
- 1/2 teaspoon salt
- Glaze
- 1/3 cup lemon juice
- 2 1/2 cups confectioners' sugar
- 2 tablespoons heavy cream

DIRECTIONS:

1. Bring the temperature of your oven to 400 F. with a piece of parchment paper, line a baking sheet
2. Place salt, flour, sugar, baking powder, cardamom, and lemon zest in the bowl of a food processor and pulse one or two times to mix. Add cold cannabis-infused butter and pulse a few times until the mixture forms coarse crumbs. Blend in the cream and pulse a few times just until incorporated. Remove dough from food processor and place in a large bowl. Fold in berries. Gather dough into a disc, wrap in plastic wrap, and refrigerate for at least 30 minutes. To cut in butter and dry ingredients using a dough scraper, then mix in cream by hand before folding in berries.
3. Roll dough to about 1/2-inch thickness on a lightly floured surface. Use a three 1/2-inch round cutter to cut out circles. Place on the prepared baking sheet. The scones must be brushed with butter or cream and bake for about 15 minutes or until tops are lightly browned. Let cool completely before applying the glaze.
4. Prepare glaze by mixing lemon juice, confectioners' sugar and heavy cream until smooth. Pour glaze over cooled scones.
5. Freezer Friendly!

Wrap fresh baked glazed scones individually in plastic wrap, place in a plastic freezer bag, and freeze. Bring to room temperature and enjoy.

Nutrition: Calories: 241, Fat: 2.9g, Fiber: 4g, Carbs: 56g, Protein: 0.81g

CHOCOLATE COCONUT PECAN PIE

Preparation Time: 15-20 minutes **- Cooking Time:** 30 minutes **- Servings:** 8-10

INGREDIENTS:

- ¼ cup melted cannabutter
- ¾ cup of sugar
- 2¼ teaspoons vanilla extract
- 3 eggs slightly beaten
- 3 tablespoons all-purpose flour
- 6 ounces sweetened dark
- chocolate bar, finely chopped
- ½ cup chopped pecans
- ½ cup shredded unsweetened
- coconut
- 9-inch prepared piecrust
- Whipped cream for topping

DIRECTIONS:

1. Preheat your oven to 350°.In a bowl, put in sugar, melted cannabutter, and vanilla extract. Mix it well, and then add in the flour and the eggs gradually...Ensure it is combined thoroughly. Fold in the pecan nuts, chocolate and coconut. Next, pour the mixture into the prepared piecrust and bake for around 30 minutes. The pie will rise during baking. After baking, let it cool in a rack, and when done, serve it with whipped cream on top.

Nutrition: Calories: 221, Fat: 5.6g, Fiber: 1.4g, Carbs: 41.7, Protein: 0.76g

STONED GUMMIES

Preparation Time: 15-20 minutes **- Cooking Time:** 5 minutes **- Servings:** 30 pcs

INGREDIENTS:

- Nonstick cooking spray
- 1 large packet (6 ounces) Jell-O, your preferred flavor
- Four ¼-ounce envelopes unflavored gelatin

- ½ cup of cold water
- ¼ cup Cannabis Tincture
- Cornstarch, for dusting
- Special equipment: silicone gummy molds, funnel or dropper

DIRECTIONS:

1. Grease the molds lightly with the cooking spray, then wipe with a paper towel, so very little oil remains. Place the molds on a rimmed baking sheet. In a small saucepan, whisk the Jell-O and gelatin together, then add the cold water and whisk to combine. Over medium heat, bring Jell-O mixture to a boil, then reduce heat to low and cook for 5 minutes, stirring often. Remove it from heat and let cool slightly. Add the tincture and mix well. Using a funnel or dropper, fill the molds. Place the baking sheet in the fridge and let chill for 15 minutes. Pop the gummies out of the molds and dust lightly with cornstarch to prevent sticking. Prolong its shelf life by Storing them in a glass container in the fridge.

Nutrition: Calories: 128, Fat: 2.7g, Fiber: 1g, Carbs: 29.9g, Protein: 0.4g

GANJA TOFFEE CHEWS

Preparation Time: 15- minutes **- Cooking Time:** 15 minutes **- Servings:** 24, pcs.

INGREDIENTS:

- 2 packs of saltine crackers
- 8 ounces of cannabutter
- 1 cup dark brown sugar
- 2 cups some flavor of confection chips semi-sweet, raspberry chocolate etc.
- 3/4 cup chopped nuts of your choice, depending on your flavor of chips.

DIRECTIONS:

1. First, line a half-size baking pan with 1 inch's sides with foil. Use a cooking spray to grease the foil and evenly distribute it, in a single layer, the saltine crackers, so they are covering the bottom of the pan but not overlapping. Also, preheat the oven to 350° and make sure the rack is in the center position. Into a heavy-bottomed saucepan, add the medicated butter and the sugar. When the mixture is already boiling, time it for exactly 3 minutes and then remove from the heat.

 Quickly pour the molten mixture over the saltines and spread to cover crackers completely. Bake in the oven for 10 minutes. Remove the pan from the oven and expect that during the baking process, the mixture bubbled and probably put the crackers in wonky positions, but that's okay. Just poke them around with a fork to realign them. When they straighten out, pour the morsels over the candy and let it rest for a few minutes while it melts. Spread the melted morsels over the entire pan and top with chopped nuts. Let cool, or if you are in a hurry, stick them in the freezer for a while! I keep individual medicated pieces wrapped and frozen. They are excellent on ice cream or alone.

Nutrition: Calories: 134, Fat: 2.1g, Fiber: 3g, Carbs: 47.6g, Protein: 0.7g

JUANITA'S CANNA LOLLIPOP

Preparation Time: 5 minutes **- Cooking Time:** 20 minutes **- Servings:** 2

INGREDIENTS:

- 1 tbsp. cannabis tincture
- 1 cup of sugar
- 1/2 cup light corn syrup
- 1/4 cup of water
- 1 teaspoon of lemon extract or other flavors

DIRECTIONS:

1. In a medium saucepan, add sugar, light corn syrup, 1/4 cup of water. Slowly heat your pan until you reach 300F while beating the whole process. Remove from the fire. Add your extract and cannabis tincture. Beat well so that your tincture is distributed in the mixture. Set up your lollipop shape and lollipop sticks. Pour the blend prepared molds and allow them to cool.

Nutrition: Calories: 125, Fat: 2.1g, Fiber: 1g, Carbs: 29.4g, Protein: 0.2g

CANNA MINT PATTIES

Preparation Time: 15 minutes to 4 hrs. for cooling **- Cooking Time:** 0 minutes **- Servings:** 24 pcs

INGREDIENTS:

- ½ cup of light corn syrup
- 2 teaspoon of peppermint extract
- ½ cup of softened cannabutter
- 2 drops of food coloring (optional)
- 9 cups of sifted powdered sugar (about 2 pounds)

DIRECTIONS:

1. Use a mixing bowl to mix the corn syrup, peppermint extract, and slightly melted Baked Butter or margarine. Then add the sugar, a little bit at a time, and incorporate it into the mix. Add the amount of food coloring to achieve your desired color and blend well.

2. Roll this mixture into small balls. Place them a few inches apart from each other on a baking sheet that has been lined with wax paper. Use a fork to make each one flat.

3. Let the mint patties set in the refrigerator for several hours. Remove the patties from the refrigerator and let stand at room temperature for several days to dry out. After a few days, when the patties are dried out, transfer them to a container with an airtight lid and store them in the refrigerator. You'll make about

24 patties. Eat 3 to 4 patties per (regular size) person to get baked.
Nutrition: Calories: 140, Fat: 2.g, Fiber: 1.7g, Carbs: 41g, Protein: 0.9g

TROPICAL ORANGE CHEWS

Preparation Time: 20 minutes **- Cooking Time:** 25-30 minutes **- Servings:** 24 pcs

INGREDIENTS:

- ½ cup of cannabutter
- 2 cups of brown sugar
- 2 slightly beaten eggs
- 2 teaspoons of vanilla
- 3 teaspoons of freshly grated orange rind
- 1 cup of flour
- 1 teaspoon of salt
- 2 teaspoons of baking powder
- 2 cups of shredded coconut
- 2 cups of chopped dates

DIRECTIONS:

1. Preheat oven to 350° F. Grease a 9 by 9-inch pan.
2. In a saucepan, melt the Baked Butter or margarine then remove the saucepan from the heat. Stir in the brown sugar, vanilla, and orange rind. Once those ingredients are well combined, add the eggs. In a bowl or on a piece of waxed paper, combine the dry ingredients. Make sure to sift the dry ingredient at least three times. Mix the wet and dry ingredients together until completely mixed. Pour the batter into a prepared baking dish. Bake for 25 to 30 minutes. Cut into 16 squares when thoroughly cooled. If you like, roll each square into a ball and roll in more coconut. One to one and a half pieces/squares/balls will get you baked.

Nutrition: Calories: 130, Fat: 2.7g, Fiber: 1g, Carbs: 31g, Protein: 0.3g

MARY JANE'S PEANUT BUTTER CUPS

Preparation Time: 1 hr. or overnight **- Cooking Time:** 0 minutes **- Servings:** 24 cups

INGREDIENTS:

- 1 cup unsalted toasted almonds
- 1 cup pitted dates
- 2 tablespoons cocoa powder

* 1 tablespoon cannabutter
* ½ cup peanut or cashew butter
* 1 tablespoon almond flour
* 1 cup semisweet chocolate chips, melted
* 2 tablespoons canna oil
* ½ teaspoon almond extract
* 1 teaspoon vanilla extract
* Sparkling sugar, for finishing

DIRECTIONS:

1. Prepare your muffin tray by putting liners on it. By the utilization of a blender or food processor, blend together dates, almonds cocoa powder, and CBD butter and pulse until it holds together. Press about 1 tablespoon of the almond mixture into the bottom of each cupcake liner. In a small bowl, combine the peanut butter and almond flour. Spread about 1 teaspoon of the peanut butter mixture on top of each cup. Put the tray in the chiller until the peanut mixture is firm. Meanwhile, in a small bowl, mix the chocolate chips, oil, and extracts. Remove the tin from the freezer and carefully spoon about 1½ teaspoons of the chocolate over each cup and smooth to the edges. Sprinkle with the sparkling sugar, freeze until firm, and enjoy.

Nutrition: Calories: 135, Fat: 2.5g, Fiber: 1.4g, Carbs: 31.5g, Protein: 0.3g

CHOCOLATE COVERED CHERRIES

Preparation Time: 1 ½ hr. **- Cooking Time:** 5 minutes **- Servings:** 12

INGREDIENTS:

* 24 cherries with stems (remove the pits or use dried ones)
* 1 cup milk chocolate chips
* 1 cup dark chocolate chips
* ¼ cup of cannabis coconut oil

DIRECTIONS:

1. In a microwave-safe bowl, heat dark chocolate chips, milk chocolate chips and cannabis coconut oil. Heat the mix for 20-seconds intervals and stir by turns until it has finally melted. Ensure the chocolate is not too hot. Cover the cherries with chocolate, and let the excess chocolate drip. Set the cherries onto a wax-lined paper. Once all the cherries are done, transfer them into the refrigerator for 1-hour Double coat the cherries if you want (transfer into the refrigerator again) Enjoy!

Nutrition: Calories: 210, Fat: 4g, Fiber: 2.1g, Carbs: 35g, Protein: 0.8g

CANNA CHOCOLATE TRUFFLES

Preparation Time: 15-20 minutes - **Cooking Time:** 0 minutes - **Servings:** 10-12

INGREDIENTS:

- ½ cup cannabutter softened
- ½cup powdered sugar
- ¼cup unsweetened cocoa powder
- ½cup almond flour
- Large pinch salt
- Dash almond extract
- Dash vanilla extract
- 24whole almonds, toasted in cannabutter and Salt
- 1cup unsweetened shredded coconut

DIRECTIONS:

1. Line a baking sheet with parchment paper. In a bowl, put all the prepared ingredients except the whole almonds and coconut and mix gently until the mixture is fairly smooth. Roll teaspoons of the mixture between your palms into balls. (Work quickly, as the butter gets very soft quickly. Refrigerate for a few minutes if the mixture gets too soft.) If using the toasted almonds, tuck one into the center of each and roll again quickly to smooth things over. Place the coconut in a bowl and roll the balls in the coconut until coated. Place on the baking sheet and refrigerate to firm up. Store the munchies in a glass container in the fridge.

Nutrition: Calories: 141, Fat: 2.1g, Fiber: 1.4g, Carbs: 31.5g, Protein: 0.2g

MARIJUANA FUDGE MUNCHIES

Preparation Time: 10 minutes - **Cooking Time:** 0 minutes - **Servings:** 6-8

INGREDIENTS:

- 1/2 Cup cannabutter
- 1/2 Cup Almond Butter
- 1/8 to 1/4 cup Honey
- 1/2 of a Banana, Mashed
- 1 tsp. Vanilla Extract
- any kind of nut butter
- 1/8 Cup Dried Fruit
- 1/8 Cup Chocolate Chips

DIRECTIONS:

1. In a blender or food processer, add in all the ingredients. Blend for several minutes until smooth.
2. Pour the batter into a loaf pan with the lining of baking paper. For larger chunks, use a mini loaf pan or double the recipe. Refrigerate or freeze until firm. Cut into 8 equal squares.

Nutrition: Calories: 210, Fat: 2.9g, Fiber: 1.7g, Carbs: 31.9g, Protein: 0.4g

OAT MUNCHIES SPHERES

Preparation Time: 20 minutes - **Cooking Time:** 5 minutes - **Servings:** 6-8

INGREDIENTS:

- 3 cups of rolled oats
- 2 tablespoons of cocoa powder
- 1 ½ cups of cannabis-infused butter
- 3 tablespoons of honey
- ¼ cup of peanut butter

DIRECTIONS:

1. Place a saucepan over heat and add cannabis-infused butter to melt. Add all other ingredients to the pan; stir and cook for 5 minutes. Pour the mixture in a baking pan and refrigerate for 15 minutes. Roll the mixture into small balls and refrigerate again. Serve.

Nutrition: Calories: 125, Fat: 1.2g, Fiber: 5g, Carbs: 38g, Protein: 1g

PAVLOV WITH CANNA-RASPBERRY SAUCE

Preparation Time: 20 minutes - **Cooking Time:** 30 minutes - **Servings:** 6

INGREDIENTS:

- For the meringues
- 3 large egg whites, at room temperature
- ½ teaspoon cream of tartar
- Pinch salt
- ⅔ cup granulated sugar
- 2 teaspoons cornstarch
- 1 teaspoon white vinegar
- 1 teaspoon vanilla extract
- For the raspberry sauce
- ½ cup of orange juice

- 2 teaspoons cornstarch
- pound raspberries, rinsed
- ¼ cup honey
- 1 tablespoon Canna-Coconut Oil
- Pinch salt

DIRECTIONS:

1. Preheat the oven to 275°F. Line a baking sheet with parchment paper. For the meringues, in a tall, metal bowl, using an electric mixer on high speed, whip the egg whites, cream of tartar, and salt together until soft peaks form, about a minute. As you are running the mixer, gradually add the sugar, 2 tablespoons at a time. Continue to beat on high speed until stiff peaks form. If you feel the meringue between your fingers, it should be smooth. If you still feel the sugar granules, keep beating on medium speed until the sugar has fully dissolved. Add in the cornstarch, vinegar, and vanilla and whisk to incorporate. Spoon about ½ cup of the egg white mixture for each pavlova onto the prepared baking sheet. Using a spoon, spread each into a 3-inch concave circle, with higher sides and a slight hollow in the middle. You should have enough for 6 pavlovas.

2. Bake until very light tan in color, and the meringue seems set, 25 to 30 minutes. Turn off the oven, open the door a smidge, and allow the pavlovas to cool completely. For the raspberry sauce, in a small bowl, combine the orange juice and cornstarch. Stir to until smooth. Over low heat, in a small saucepan, combine the raspberries, honey, and canna-oil and mix well, mashing the raspberries into a smooth sauce as they soften. Add the cornstarch mixture, increase the heat to medium, and stir until the mixture begins to thicken, 4 to 5 minutes; the sauce will continue to thicken as it cools. Stir in the salt. Put it away from the heat and pour into a small pitcher. Top the pavlovas with equal portions of the raspberry sauce immediately before serving.

3. Storage: You can prepare the pavlovas hours in advance and store them in an airtight container at room temperature until ready to serve. The sauce can also be made in advance and stored in the refrigerator, covered. If the consistency is too thick and hard to pour, heat it in the microwave for 10 seconds or so. Once sauced, you need to eat the pavlovas immediately.

Nutrition: Calories: 215, Fat: 2.7g, Fiber: 1.7g, Carbs: 53g, Protein: 1.2g

CHOCOLATE OLIVE OIL CAKE

Preparation Time: 15 minutes - **Cooking Time:** 30 minutes - **Servings:** 6-8

INGREDIENTS:

- 3 cups all-purpose flour
- 2 cups of sugar
- 6 tablespoons good-quality cocoa powder

- 2 teaspoons baking soda
- 1 teaspoon salt
- ½ cup finely chopped nuts or dried fruit (optional)
- ¾ cup canna oil
- 2 tablespoons white vinegar
- 1tablespoon vanilla
- 2 cups cold water Powdered sugar, for dusting

DIRECTIONS:

1. Preheat the oven to 350°F. Grease and flour two 8-inch cake pans or lines a 12-cup muffin tin with muffin liners. In a bowl, put in sugar and flour, cocoa powder, baking soda, salt, and nuts or dried fruit (if using). Whisk to incorporate. In another bowl, whisk together the oil, vinegar, vanilla, and water, then add to the flour mixture. With a hand mixer on medium-low speed, mix just until smooth. Pour into the prepared cake pans or muffin tin. Bake 30 to 40 minutes for cake or 20 to 25 minutes for muffins, or until a toothpick inserted in the center comes out clean (start checking early to avoid over baking). Cool completely. Before serving, dust with powdered sugar.

Nutrition: Calories: 210, Fat:6.8g, Fiber: 4.1, Carbs: 34.6g, Protein: 2.1g

ORANGE ALMOND CAKE

Preparation Time: 15 minutes - **Cooking Time:** 45-50 minutes - **Servings:** 6-8

INGREDIENTS:

- 2 cups packed almond flour, plus more for dusting
- 1 teaspoon baking powder
- ½ teaspoon baking soda
- 1 teaspoon ground cinnamon
- 1 teaspoon ground ginger
- ½ teaspoon salt
- 3 eggs, lightly beaten⅔ cup honey plus1 teaspoon, divided
- ¼ cup canna oil
- Zest and juice (¼ cup) of 1 orange
- 1 cup fresh raspberries
- Whipped cream, chopped toasted almonds or pistachios, and powdered sugar, for garnish

DIRECTIONS:

1. Preheat the oven to 325°F. Grease a 9-inch spring form pan and dust the inside with almond flour. In a large bowl, whisk together the almond flour, baking powder, baking soda, cinnamon, ginger, and salt. In another bowl, whisk together the eggs, ⅔ cup of the honey, oil, and orange zest. The dry

ingredients will then be added to the egg mixture and fold in until just a few lumps remain, then gently fold in the raspberries. Put the mixture in the prepared pan and smoothen the top part. Bake for 45 to 50 minutes, or until the edges are browned, and the center is set. Warm the remaining 1 teaspoon honey with the orange juice. Brush this onto the warm cake—it'll sink right in—then let it cool completely in the pan. To serve, garnish slices with whipped cream, chopped almonds or pistachios, and a dusting of powdered sugar.

Nutrition: Calories: 219, Fat:5.8g, Fiber: 6.4, Carbs: 32.1g, Protein: 3.2g

CRANBERRY BREAD

Preparation Time: 15 minutes - **Cooking Time:** 50-60 minutes - **Servings:** 6-8

INGREDIENTS:

- 2 cups of the gluten-free flour mix
- 1 teaspoon of salt
- 5 teaspoons of baking powder
- 2 teaspoons of gelatin
- ½ cup of cannabutter
- ½ cup of sugar
- 3 eggs, separated
- ½ tablespoon of grated orange rind
- ¾ cup of orange juice (fresh squeezed is best)
- 1 cup of fresh cranberries, cut in half

DIRECTIONS:

1. Bring the temperature of your oven to 350. Ensure to grease and flour an 8 x 8-inch loaf pan (glass is best).

2. In a medium bowl, whisk together the gluten-free flour, salt, baking powder (gluten-free), and gelatin gum, using a wire whisk. Using a mixer set on medium-high, cream the Cannabutter or margarine and sugar until fluffy. Add the egg yolks and beat on medium-high until combined. Next, add the orange rind and then a little of the flour. Mix. Add orange juice. Mix. Repeat this process until all the flour and juice are mixed. Stir in the cranberries using a wooden spoon. Beat the egg whites until stiff and then fold them gently into the batter. Pour in the batter onto the prepared pan then place it in the center of the oven. Bake for about 50 minutes, 60 if needed. The loaf should be golden in color. When cool, cut the loaf into 12 slices. One slice should do the trick. For an extra zing spread, Cannabutter or margarine on the slice before eating.

Nutrition: Calories: 229, Fat:5.5g, Fiber: 5g, Carbs: 39g, Protein: 4g

CANNA-BANANA BREAD

Preparation Time: 10-15 minutes - **Cooking Time:** 60 minutes - **Servings:** 4-6

INGREDIENTS:

- ½ cup of soft Cannabutter
- 1 cup of white sugar
- 2 eggs
- 1 teaspoon of vanilla extract
- 1 ½ cup of mashed banana
- 2 cups of flour
- 1 teaspoon of baking soda

DIRECTIONS:

1. Preheat the oven to 350 degrees. Grease a 9 "x 5" loaf tin and dust with flour. Beat the Cannabutter and the sugar until smooth. Add vanilla extract. Beat in the eggs and then the bananas. Stir in flour and baking powder carefully. Pour the bread batter into the pan. Bake in the preheated oven for an hour.

Nutrition: Calories: 295, Fat:8.1g, Fiber: 2.3, Carbs: 45g, Protein: 1.8g

RED VELVET CANNA CAKE

Preparation Time: 20 minutes - **Cooking Time:** 35-40 minutes - **Servings:** 20-24

INGREDIENTS:

- 16 ounces of cream cheese
- 4 ounces of butter, softened
- 3 cups of powdered sugar
- 2 ¾ cup of purpose flour
- 1 ¾ cup of white sugar
- 1 ¼ cup of buttermilk
- ¾ cup of canola oil
- ¾ cup canna oil
- 2 eggs
- 1 tablespoon of white vinegar
- 4 teaspoons of red food coloring
- 3 teaspoons of vanilla extract
- 2 teaspoons of cocoa powder
- 1 teaspoon of baking soda

- ¼ teaspoon of salt

DIRECTIONS:

1. Before you do anything preheat the oven to 325 F. Beat the eggs with canna oil, canola oil, 1 teaspoon of vanilla extract, buttermilk and vinegar in a large mixing bowl Stir the flour with white sugar, cocoa powder, baking soda and salt. Add the mixture gradually to the buttermilk while whisking all the time until no lumps are found. Add the liquid food coloring and stir in the batter until you get a dark red batter. Pour the batter into 3 lined up and greased cake pans then cook them in the oven for 34 to 36 min. Once the time is up, allow the cakes to lose heat completely. In the meantime, beat the butter in a large mixing bowl until they become soft. Add the sugar gradually while beating all the time, followed by the cream cheese until the mix becomes soft and fluffy. Add the vanilla extract then mix them well to make the icing. Level the cakes with a sharp bread knife to make them equal with the same thickness and size. Place some icing in the middle of a cake stand and place it on top of it a cake. Spread some frosting on it, then top it with the second cake and repeat the process to with the third cake. Cover the whole cake with the rest of the frosting, then decorate it the way you desire and refrigerate it for 30 min or more. Serve your cake and enjoy it.

Nutrition: Calories: 288, Fat:8.7g, Fiber: 2.1g, Carbs: 54g, Protein: 1.8g

CHERRY- CRANBERRY GINGER CAKE

Preparation Time: 15 minutes - **Cooking Time:** 35 -40 minutes - **Servings:** 4-6

INGREDIENTS:

- 1½ cups Dark Cherries drained, chopped-set aside
- 2 cups whole wheat white cake flour
- ½ teaspoon ground ginger
- 2 tablespoons chopped crystallized ginger
- ¼ teaspoon salt
- 1½ teaspoons baking powder
- ½ cup cranberries
- ½ cup apricots, chopped
- ¾ cup canna milk
- 2 eggs
- ¼ cup stevia
- 3 tablespoons molasses
- ¼ cup coconut oil softened

DIRECTIONS:

1. Prepare a lightly greased and lined with parchment paper 9-inch cake pan. In a bowl, put all dry

ingredients together and mix well. Then, in another bowl, put all wet ingredients and mix with a whisk. Combine egg mixture and flour and blend Fold in cherries and bake at 350°F for 30-35 minutes.

Nutrition: Calories: 256, Fat:6.5g, Fiber: 4g, Carbs: 41.2g, Protein: 1.7g

PEACH JELLY ROLL

Preparation Time: 15-20 minutes   **- Cooking Time:** 60 minutes **- Servings:** 6-8

INGREDIENTS:

- 2¼ cups whole wheat pastry flour
- ¼ cup wheat bran, unprocessed
- ½ teaspoon baking powder
- ¼ teaspoon baking soda
- ½ teaspoon salt
- ½ cup canna coconut oil, slightly softened but still firm
- ¾ cup yogurt
- ¼ cup milk
- 8 cups peaches, thinly sliced
- 1 cup dates, minced
- ¼ cup honey

DIRECTIONS:

1. In a bowl, combine all the prepared dry ingredients and mix well. Mix in coconut oil and slowly add other wet ingredients except for peaches, dates and honey, for the remaining three ingredients, mix all of it and set aside. Divide dough in two and roll each on a floured surface into a rectangle shape
2. Split peaches in half and top each section of rolled dough, leaving edges free. Roll up without letting peaches fall out and pinch to seal. In a greased pan, bake, covered at 350°F for 30 minutes and uncovered for an additional 30 minutes.

Nutrition: Calories: 210, Fat:6.8g, Fiber: 4.1, Carbs: 34.6g, Protein: 2.1g

SILKY COCONUT CAKE

Preparation Time: 15-20 minutes **- Cooking Time:** 30-40 minutes **- Servings:** 6-8

INGREDIENTS:

- 2 cups whole wheat cake flour
- 2 teaspoons baking powder
- ½ cup toasted wheat bran

- ½ teaspoon baking soda
- 3 teaspoons lemon zest
- ½ cup of cocoa powder
- ½ teaspoon salt
- 2 large eggs
- ½ cup molasses
- ½ cup dark honey
- ½ cup apple juice
- ½ cup of coconut oil at room temperature
- ¾ cup dark chocolate chips
- Chocolate Frosting (optional)

DIRECTIONS:

1. In a bowl, combine all the prepared dry ingredients and mix well. Same goes with all the wet ingredients, slowly add together using whisk; egg mixture, flour mixture and 1 cup boiling water, a little at a time until totally incorporated; do not over mix Stir in chocolate chips then fold. Pour cake in a lined 12-inch round spring form pan and bake at 350°F for 30-40 minutes until springs back when you press. Cool then frost with chocolate frosting.

Nutrition: Calories: 245, Fat:8g, Fiber: 4.3g, Carbs: 30.9g, Protein: 2.6g

CANNABIS STRAWBERRY CAKE

Preparation Time: 20 minutes - **Cooking Time:** 40 minutes - **Servings:** 12

INGREDIENTS:

- Nonstick baking spray
- 10 tablespoons (1¼ sticks) unsalted butter,
- 2 tablespoons Canna-Butter, melted
- 1¼ cups plus 2 tablespoons granulated sugar, divided
- 2 large eggs, lightly beaten
- 1 tablespoon orange juice concentrate
- 2 teaspoons grated orange zest
- ½ teaspoon almond extract
- 1½ cups gluten-free 1-to-1 baking flour
- ½ cup plus 1 tablespoon strawberry jam, divided
- 1 cup slivered or sliced almonds
- 1½ cups vanilla Greek yogurt

DIRECTIONS:

1. Preheat the oven to 340°F.Using a nonstick spray or butter and flour, Coat a 9-inch square baking pan. In a large bowl, combine the melted butter and 1¼ cups of sugar. Stir in the beaten eggs and mix well. Stir in the orange juice concentrate, zest, and almond extract. Stir in the flour until just mixed. Pour the batter into the prepared pan. Using a knife, swirl ½ cup of the jam into the batter toward the center. Sprinkle with the almonds, then the remaining 2 tablespoons sugar. Bake until golden and set, 35 to 40 minutes. Once completely cooled slice into 12 equal pieces. In a small bowl, combine the yogurt with the remaining 1 tablespoon jam and place a dollop on each slice.

Nutrition: Calories: 341, Fat:8.1g, Fiber: 6g, Carbs: 41.7g, Protein: 1.7g

STONER'S LEMON POPPY SEED LOAF

Preparation Time: 20 minutes - **Cooking Time:** 55-65 min - **Servings:** 6-8

INGREDIENTS:

- 1 ¾ cups All-purpose flour
- ¾ cup Cannabis Butter* melted
- 1 tablespoon poppy seeds
- 1 cup Granulated sugar
- 1 teaspoon Baking powder
- 2/3 cup Milk
- 2 Eggs 1 teaspoon Vanilla
- 1 tablespoon Lemon zest
- ½ teaspoon Salt
- For the Glaze
- ½ cup icing sugar
- 1 tablespoon Lemon juice

DIRECTIONS:

1. Preheat oven the oven to 350 F. Grease a 9 × 5 in. Loaf pan. Mix flour with sugar, poppy seeds, lemon zest, baking powder and salt in a bowl. Cream the Cannabis Butter* with milk, eggs and vanilla in a large bowl, using a whisk or an electric mixer on medium, until smooth and creamy in texture, Then, blend in flour mixture and mix until just combined. Don't over-mix. Pour the mixture into a loaf pan. Bake and check if it is cooked by inserting a wooden skewer or toothpick in the center of the loaf and when it comes out clean, around 55 to 65 min. Transfer pan to a cooling rack, and let stand 10 min. Meanwhile, do the glaze, Whisk icing sugar with lemon juice in a small bowl. Brush glaze over warm loaf. Let stand until loaf is cool, about 2 hours.

Nutrition: Calories: 290, Fat:3.5, Fiber: 4.1, Carbs: 45g, Protein: 4.6g

CHOCO-ESPRESSO SPELT CAKE

Preparation Time: 30 minutes - **Cooking Time:** 1 hr. - **Servings:** 8-12

INGREDIENTS:

- 2 cups spelt flour
- 3/4 cup cannabutter
- 3/4 cup cocoa powder
- 1 cup packed dark brown sugar
- 2 large eggs
- 1 cup boiling-hot water
- 1 1/2 tablespoons instant espresso powder
- 1 teaspoon baking soda
- 1 1/2 cups dates (12 to 14), pitted and coarsely chopped
- 2 teaspoons baking powder
- 3/4 teaspoon salt
- 1 1/2 teaspoons vanilla extract

DIRECTIONS:

1. Preheat oven to 350F. Grease spring form pan, then lightly dust with cocoa powder, removing out excess. Mix together boiling-hot water, espresso powder, vanilla, and baking soda in a bowl, then add dates, mashing lightly with a fork, and slightly simmer then cool down to room temperature, about 10 minutes. Blend together spelt flour, cocoa powder, baking powder, and salt in another bowl. Cream together canna butter and brown sugar until pale and fluffy. Put in the eggs one at a time. Add in date mixture and add the flour a little at a time, mixing until just combined. Spoon batter into a spring form pan, smoothing top, and bake until a wooden pick or skewer inserted into the center comes out clean, about 50 minutes to 1 hour. Cool down the cake by transferring it to a rack for a few minutes, then remove side of the pan and cool cake on rack. Serve cake warm or at room temperature.

Nutrition: Calories: 280, Fat:6.1g, Fiber: 4.3g, Carbs: 39.1g, Protein: 5g

CANNA CINNAMON COFFEE CAKE

Preparation Time: 20 minutes - **Cooking Time:** 30 minutes - **Servings:** 4-6

INGREDIENTS:

- 1 1/4 cups flour (cannabis flour extra potency)
- 1/4 cup cannabutter
- 1/2 cup sugar

- 1/4 cup sour cream
- 1/3 cup canna milk or regular milk
- 2 eggs, slightly beaten
- 2 tsp. baking powder
- 1.5 tsp. cinnamon
- Topping:
- 1/3 cup flour
- 1/3 cup brown sugar
- 1/4 cup cannabutter
- 1 tsp. cinnamon powder

DIRECTIONS:

1. First, preheat the oven to375 degrees Fahrenheit, subsequently combining all ingredients for the cake batter in a large mixing bowl. After thoroughly mixing, pour the batter into an 8 or 9-inch greased or buttered pan. After this, combine the flour and brown sugars for the topping in a big bowl, mixing in the cannabutter and cinnamon after. Mix until it becomes chunky and crumbly. Spread over the batter and bake for 28-30 minutes.

Nutrition: Calories: 311, Fat:7,5g, Fiber: 3g, Carbs: 40.1g, Protein: 5g

CANNA APPLE PECAN SPACE CAKE

Preparation Time: 20 minutes - **Cooking Time:** 45 minutes - **Servings:** 4-6

INGREDIENTS:

- 1 cup flour
- 1/2 cup whole wheat flour
- 1/4 tsp. cinnamon
- 1/2 tsp. baking soda
- 1/2 tsp. nutmeg
- 1/2 tsp. salt
- 1 egg
- 1 cup granulated
- 2/3 cup canna oil
- 1/2 cup pecans chopped
- 2 apples, peeled and grated
- 1 gala apple, thinly sliced
- 15 pecan halves

For the glaze:

- 1/4 cup brown sugar
- 2 tsp. cannabis oil
- 2 tsp. water

DIRECTIONS:

1. Heat your oven to 325 degrees Fahrenheit. Lightly coat a 9-inch spring form pan with nonstick cooking spray, In a medium bowl, combine the cinnamon, flours, baking soda, nutmeg and salt until blended. Whisk sugar and egg with the 2/3 cup cannabis-infused olive oil in a bowl. Stir the flour mixture into the egg mixture, and add the chopped pecans and grated apples. Scrape into the prepared pan and flatten the top of it, Arrange the apple slices on top of the edge of the cake, and arrange the pecan halves in one layer in the center.

2. Make the glaze in a small bowl. Mix together the brown sugar and the 2 tsp. olive oil and water and microwave in thirty-second intervals until the brown sugar is melted. Brush the apples and pecan with half of the glaze and save the rest.

3. Bake in the center of the oven until a toothpick when inserted in the middle of the cake comes out clean. Remove the pan out of the oven and brush the top of the warm cake with the rest of the glaze. Gently remove the cake from the base then serve.

Nutrition: Calories: 290, Fat:7.2g, Fiber: 4.1, Carbs: 46g, Protein: 3.4g

CANNA CARROT MUFFINS

Preparation Time: 15 minutes - **Cooking Time:** 25-30 minutes - **Servings:** 10-12

INGREDIENTS:

- 1¾ cups flour
- 1 teaspoon salt
- 1 teaspoon cinnamon
- 1teaspoon ground ginger
- ½ teaspoon grated nutmeg
- ¼ teaspoon baking soda
- ⅛ teaspoon baking powder
- 1 cup maple syrup
- ½ cup solid CBD Coconut Oil melted, or ¼ cup CBD Oil mixed with ¼ cup vegetable oil
- ½ cup milk
- 1 tablespoon fresh lemon juice
- 1 teaspoon vanilla extract
- 2 cups grated carrot
- ½ cup crushed pineapple, drained

- ½ cup each raisin, coconut, and pecans (or any nuts you like)

DIRECTIONS:

1. Preheat the oven to 350°F. Line two 12-cup muffin tins with muffin papers or grease and flour the tins. In a large bowl, combine the flour, salt, cinnamon, ginger, nutmeg, baking soda, and baking powder. In a separate bowl, combine the maple syrup, coconut oil, milk, lemon juice, and vanilla. Combine both the wet and dry ingredients then fold it gently until just combined (over mixing makes the muffins tough). Fold in the carrots, pineapple, raisins, coconut, and pecans. Fill the prepared muffin tins two-thirds full. Let the cake bake for around 25 minutes or more or until a toothpick inserted into the center of a muffin comes out clean. Let them cool a little before serving.

Nutrition: Calories: 200, Fat:5.1g, Fiber: 2tgg, Carbs: 25.8g, Protein: 1.2g

RUM RAISIN CUPCAKES

INGREDIENTS:

- Rum Raisins
- ¼ cup dark rum
- ½ cup golden raisins
- Cupcakes
- 1 cup all-purpose flour
- 1¼ teaspoons baking powder
- ¼ teaspoon ground cinnamon
- ⅛ teaspoon ground allspice
- ⅛ teaspoon freshly grated nutmeg
- ½ cup cannabutter, slightly softened
- 2 tablespoons unsalted butter, slightly softened
- ¾ cup firmly packed light brown sugar
- 3 large eggs
- 1 tablespoon pure vanilla extract
- ¼ teaspoon pure rum extract
- Sweet Cream Frosting
- ¼ cup unsalted butter, slightly softened
- ½ cup heavy cream
- 2 cups powdered sugar, sifted
- ⅛ teaspoon salt

DIRECTIONS:

1. Prepare the rum raisins: In a small saucepan, warm the rum over low heat. Blend in the raisins and

put it away from heat. Put the mix in a bowl, and then cover it with a saran wrap and let sit at room temperature for at least 6 hours or overnight. Prepare the cupcakes: Bring the temperature of your oven to 180c Put paper liners in the muffin tin. Ina medium bowl, stir together the flour, baking powder, cinnamon, allspice, and nutmeg. Set aside. Ina large bowl using an electric mixer, beat together the cannabutter, regular butter, and brown sugar on medium to high speed until you see that it becomes light and cloudlike, gradually add eggs, beating well after each addition. Beat in the vanilla and rum extracts. Reduce the speed mixer to low, add the flour mixture, and mix until just combined. Fold in the rum raisins and any remaining liquid. Scoop up the cupcake batter into the pan. Bake it for about 20 to 25 minutes, or until golden brown and a toothpick inserted into the center of a cupcake comes out clean. Let cool in the tin for 5 minutes, and then transfer to a wire rack to cool completely. Cupcakes without frosting can be stored up to 3 months. Prepare the sweet cream frosting: In a medium bowl using an electric mixer, beat the butter on medium speed until creamy. Lower down the speed to medium and add the cream and 1 cup of the powdered sugar; beat until well combined. Slowly add the remaining1 cup sugar and the salt. Put the frosting to a piping bag fitted with the tip of your choice and frost the cupcakes, or simply frost them with a butter knife or small offset spatula. Store the frosted cupcakes in an airtight container in the refrigerator for up to 1 week.

Nutrition: Calories: 215, Fat:5g, Fiber: 4.1, Carbs: 35.6g, Protein: 2g

HOT GANJA CHOCOLATE CUPCAKES

Preparation Time: 10 minutes - **Cooking Time:** 20-25 minutes - **Servings:** 2-4
INGREDIENTS:

- ½ Cup all-purpose flour
- 1 tsp. Baking Powder
- Pinch Salt
- 1/3 Cup Cocoa
- ½-1 t Hot Red Pepper Flakes
- 2 tbsp. canna oil
- Scant ½ Cup of milk
- ½ tsp. Vanilla
- ¼ tsp. Apple Cider Vinegar
- ¼ Cup Sugar

DIRECTIONS:

1. Preheat oven to 365°. Combine Flour, Baking Powder, Salt and Sugar. Whisk! Add wet ingredients and whisk until completely smooth. Fill 4-5 cupcake liners 2/3 full. Bake for 20 minutes or until a

toothpick comes out clean. Allow to cool completely before frosting.

Nutrition: Calories: 187, Fat:4.3g, Fiber: 2g, Carbs: 29.6g, Protein: 1g

FRENCH TOAST CUPCAKES

Preparation Time: 20 minutes **- Cooking Time:** 20-25 minutes **- Servings:** 12

INGREDIENTS:

- Topping
- ¼ cup all-purpose flour
- ¼ cup of sugar
- 2½ tablespoons unsalted butter, cut into ½-inch pieces and chilled
- ½ teaspoon ground cinnamon
- ¼ cup chopped pecans
- Cupcakes
- 1½ cups all-purpose flour
- 1 cup of sugar
- 1½ teaspoons baking powder
- 1 teaspoon ground cinnamon
- ½ teaspoon ground allspice
- ¼ teaspoon freshly grated nutmeg
- ½ teaspoon salt
- ½ cup cannabutter slightly softened
- ½ cup sour cream
- 2 large eggs
- ½ teaspoon maple extract
- 4 slices bacon

DIRECTIONS:

1. First the topping must be prepared. In a medium bowl, blend in sugar, flour, cinnamon, walnuts and butter. Using your fingers, blend in the butter until there are no pieces bigger than a little pea. Cover and refrigerate until prepared to use. Set up the cupcakes: Preheat your stove to 350°F. Line a 12-cup biscuit tin with paper liners. In an enormous bowl, whisk together the flour, sugar, preparing powder, cinnamon, allspice, nutmeg, and salt. Put in a safe spot. In a huge bowl utilizing an electric blender, beat together the cannabutter, cream, eggs, and maple syrup on medium speed until the blend is mixed well. Lessen the blender speed to low and include the flour blend. Beat until simply consolidated. Fill each well of the biscuit tin 2/3 full, bake it for around 20 to 25 minutes or until a toothpick embedded into the focal point of a cupcake tells the truth. While the cupcakes are heating,

cook the bacon as how you like it done. Move to a paper towel to drip the excess oil and let cool. Cupcakes must be chilled off in the tin for around 15 minutes. At that point, move to a wire rack to cool totally. Cut the bacon into 12 pieces and press a piece into the top of each muffin. For storing muffins in the freezer, seal it tightly, and it can last up to 3 months, just omit the bacon. Reheat in the toaster oven for extra deliciousness.

Nutrition: Calories: 190, Fat:5g, Fiber: 3g, Carbs: 28.8g, Protein: 1.7g

CANNABIS HUMMINGBIRD CUPCAKES

Preparation Time: 10-15 minutes **- Cooking Time:** 15-20 minutes **- Servings:** 12

INGREDIENTS:

- 2 large ripe bananas, mashed
- 1 cup of all-purpose
- 1/2 tsp. baking powder
- 1/3 cup pineapple (crushed (do not drain)
- 1/2 tsp. baking soda
- 1/2 tsp. ground cinnamon
- 1/4 tsp. salt
- ½ cup cannabutter, at room temperature
- 1/2 cup sugar
- 2 large eggs
- 1 tsp. pure vanilla extract
- 1/2 cup chopped pecans
- 1 cup unsweetened desiccated coconut
- 1/2 cup golden raisins (optional)
- Cream Cheese Frosting
- 8 ounces cream cheese, at room temperature
- 1/4 cup butter, at room temperature
- 3 cups powdered sugar
- 2 teaspoons vanilla extract

DIRECTIONS:

1. Preheat your oven to 350 degrees placing the rack in the center. Line a 12-cup muffin pan with cupcake liners in preparation. Combine the bananas and pineapples in a bowl. Mash together with the back of a fork and set aside. Whisk or beat together the flour, baking powder, baking soda, cinnamon and salt in a separate medium bowl. Add the cannabutter and the sugar to a large bowl. Beat with a whisk until the mixture is fluffy and light. Gradually put the eggs and then the vanilla

extract. Add the dry ingredients into the wet by scoopfuls and beat until thoroughly combined.

2. Stir in the pineapple and bananas, being careful not to over-mix. Fold in the pecans, coconut and golden raisins (if using). Pour batter into the liners, working to fill at least 2/3 of the way. Put it inside the oven and let it bake for around 30 to 40 minutes. The signs of completed cupcakes will include a toothpick that comes out clean and an outwardly golden appearance.

3. Remove from the oven and place on a wire rack to cool. Once this is achieved, use a small spatula or kitchen knife to frost tops of each cupcake. Top with finely chopped pecans.

4. Frosting (Cream-cheese)

5. Put the cream cheese and the butter in a bowl then and beat together with a whisk until very smooth and no lumps. Then add in the vanilla extract and fine sugar, continuously beating until it is light and smooth.

Nutrition: Calories: 216, Fat:3.1g, Fiber: 1.4g, Carbs: 56g, Protein: 4

PUMPKIN FLAN WITH PUMPKIN SEED PRALINE

Preparation Time: 6 hrs. (For cooling) - **Cooking Time:** 1-2 hrs. - **Servings:** 4-6

INGREDIENTS:

- 1¾ cups granulated sugar
- 1 cup whole milk
- 2 (5-ounce) cans evaporated milk
- 2 tablespoons plus
- 2 teaspoons canna sugar
- 5 large eggs
- ¼ teaspoon salt
- 1¾ cups pure pumpkin puree
- 2 tablespoons tequila
- 1 tablespoon orange zest
- 2 teaspoons ground cinnamon
- 1 teaspoon ground ginger
- ¼ teaspoon ground cardamom
- ¼ teaspoon freshly grated nutmeg
- 1 tablespoon pure vanilla extract
- Pumpkin Seed Praline
- Vegetable oil, for greasing the foil

- 1 cup granulated sugar
- Pinch of salt
- ½ cup of water
- 1 cup hulled (green) pumpkin seeds, toasted

DIRECTIONS:

1. Preheat the oven to 375°F. Set a 2-quartsoufflé dish or round ceramic casserole in the middle of the oven to preheat. Using a pot, bring water to a boil. In a dry, heavy, 2-quart saucepan, heat 1 cup of the granulated sugar over medium-low heat, stirring slowly with a fork until the sugar melts and turns golden brown. Cook, without stirring, swirling the pan, until the sugar is deep amber, about 5 minutes. This is your caramel. Remove the hot soufflé dish from the oven and immediately pour the caramel into the dish, tilting it to cover the bottom and sides completely. Set it aside to harden while you prepare the rest of the flan. (Leave the oven on.) Ina medium saucepan, combine the whole milk and the evaporated milk. Bring to a gentle simmer over medium heat, and then remove from the heat. Pour the milk mixture through a fine-mesh sieve into a bowl; set aside. Ina large bowl using an electric mixer, beat together the remaining¾ cup granulated sugar, the canna sugar, and the eggs on medium speed until smooth and creamy. Beat in the salt, pumpkin, tequila, orange zest, cinnamon, ginger, cardamom, nutmeg, and vanilla. While stirring, add the strained milk mixture in a slow stream and stir until it is mixed well Pour the custard over the caramel in the dish and set the dish in a roasting pan. Put in the boiling water in the pan until it comes about 1 inch up the sides of the soufflé dish. Put the pan in the middle of the oven and reduce the oven temperature to 350°F. Bake it until the color is golden brown on top and a knife inserted into the center of the flan comes out clean, 1¼ to 1½ hours. Take the baking dish out of the water bath and transfer it to a wire rack to cool. Refrigerate at least 6 hours. Prepare the praline: Preheat the oven to 250°F. Use an aluminum foil t line a baking sheet and lightly oil the foil. Set the baking sheet in the oven to keep warm. Ina deep, heavy, 2-quart saucepan, combine the sugar, salt, and ½ cup water and cook over medium-low heat, stirring slowly with a fork, until melted and pale golden. Cook the caramel without stirring, tilting the pan from side to side, until deep golden. Immediately stir in the pumpkin seeds and quickly pour the mixture onto the prepared baking sheet, spreading it into a thin sheet before it hardens. (when the caramel becomes too solid and is difficult to spread, raise the oven temperature to 400°F and place the baking sheet in the oven until the caramel is warm enough to spread, 1 to 2 minutes.) Let the praline cool on the baking sheet on a wire rack until completely hardened, and then break it into large pieces. To unmold the flan, run a thin knife around the edges to loosen it. Wiggle the dish from side to side; when the flan moves freely in the dish, invert a large serving platter with a lip over the dish. Holding the dish and platter securely together, quickly invert them together, turning the flan out onto the platter. The caramel will pool over and around it—this is exactly what you want to happen, so don't worry—it's normal. Slice the flan into wedges and serve with the caramel spooned over it, topped with shards of the praline.

Nutrition: Calories: 289, Fat:9g, Fiber: 2.5g, Carbs: 61g, Protein: 1.8g

LEMON PANNA COTTA

Preparation Time: 20 minutes plus a cooling time of 4 hrs. - **Cooking Time:** 15 minutes - **Servings:** 6

INGREDIENTS:

- 1 envelope of unflavored gelatin
- 2 cups of Marijuana Milk
- 2 tablespoons of heavy cream
- 1/2 cup of sugar
- 2 teaspoons of pure vanilla extract
- 21/4 cups of plain yogurt (preferably Greek-style)
- 2 teaspoons of freshly squeezed lemon juice

For the Fruit Topping:

- 1 cup of raspberries, red and golden
- 2 cups of mixed strawberries or blueberries
- 2 peaches, peeled, thinly sliced
- 2 teaspoons of canna sugar
- 1 ounce of Vodka
- 1 ounce of Campari
- 1 tablespoon of lemon zest

DIRECTIONS:

1. Sprinkle the entire package of gelatin over 2 tablespoons of heavy cream in a small bowl. Let it soften for about 5 minutes. Combine the Marijuana Milk, sugar and vanilla in a saucepan over low heat. Bring this mixture to a simmer for a couple of minutes then remove the saucepan from the heat. Stir the gelatin and cream mixture in a saucepan until it's all dissolved. Place the yogurt in a medium bowl and whisk until smooth. Gradually whisk the Marijuana Milk mixture and lemon juice into the yogurt. Pour mixture into six small ramekins. Cool it in the fridge for about 4 hours or until set. For the topping, toss the fruit, Vector Vodka, Cannabis Campari and sugar together with the lemon zest. Refrigerate for at least 20 minutes. To remove the Panna Cotta from the ramekins, run a sharp knife around the edges then invert the ramekin onto a plate. Top with fruit mixture and serve.

Nutrition: Calories: 255, Fat:6g, Fiber: 2.4g, Carbs: 50.1, Protein: 0.4g

TROPICAL COCONUT PUDDING

Preparation Time: 5 minutes - **Cooking Time:** 15 minutes - **Servings:** 2

INGREDIENTS:

- ¾ cup old-fashioned gluten-free oats
- ½ cup unsweetened shredded coconut
- 2 cups of water
- 1¼ cups coconut milk
- 2 teaspoons canna-oil (here)
- ½ teaspoon ground cinnamon
- 1 banana, sliced

DIRECTIONS:

1. Using a bowl, combine the oats, coconut, and water. Cover and chill overnight. Transfer the mixture to a small saucepan. Add the milk, canna-oil, and cinnamon, and simmer for about 12 minutes over medium heat. Remove from the heat, and let stand for 5 minutes. Divide between 2 bowls and top with the banana slices.
2. If you would prefer an even tastier treat, sauté the banana slices in a little butter and brown sugar before topping the pudding.

Nutrition: Calories: 156, Fat:1,3g, Fiber: 8.9g, Carbs: 49g, Protein: 2g

HEALTHY CHIA SEED PUDDING

Preparation Time: 35 minutes plus cooling time - **Cooking Time:** 0 minutes - **Servings:** 2

INGREDIENTS:

- 1½ cups almond milk
- 8 dates, pitted and chopped
- ⅓ cup chia seeds
- ¼ cup unsweetened cocoa powder
- 4 teaspoons canna-oil (here)
- ½ teaspoon ground cinnamon

DIRECTIONS:

1. Using a bowl, combine all the ingredients. Stir well. The next step is done by covering it with saran wrap and chill in the refrigerator overnight. Transfer the mixture to a blender and pulse several times until coarse and uniform. Pour the mixture into individual pudding bowls. Cover the remaining servings with plastic wrap and store in the refrigerator for up to a week.

Nutrition: Calories: 160, Fat:2g, Fiber: 8.8g, Carbs: 51g, Protein: 2.4g

CANNA RICE PUDDING WITH RAISINS AND APRICOTS

Preparation Time: 5 minutes - **Cooking Time:** 25 minutes - **Servings:** 6

INGREDIENTS:

- 3 cups whole milk
- 3 cups cooked white rice
- 2 tablespoons canna-butter (here)
- ½ cup raisins
- ½ cup chopped dried apricots
- ⅓ cup brown sugar
- ¼ teaspoon ground cinnamon
- 2 teaspoons vanilla extract

DIRECTIONS:

1. Using a medium saucepan, combine the milk, rice, canna-butter, raisins, apricots, sugar, and cinnamon. Bring to a boil, then immediately reduce the heat. Simmer gently over low heat for 25 minutes or until the rice is tender. Stir in the vanilla. Serve warm. Store the remaining servings in an airtight container in the refrigerator for up to a week. Reheat in the microwave on low heat for 2 minutes or until warm, or enjoy chilled.

Nutrition: Calories: 251, Fat:6.1g, Fiber: 2.8g, Carbs: 53.2, Protein: 0.9g

CANNA BANANA PARFAIT

Preparation Time: 30 minutes plus cooling - **Cooking Time:** 30 minutes - **Servings:** 6

INGREDIENTS:

- 6 large egg yolks
- ¾ cup granulated sugar
- ¼ cup plus 2 tablespoons cornstarch
- ¼ heaping teaspoon salt
- 3½ cups whole milk
- 1 tablespoon unsalted cannabutter
- 1 tablespoon vanilla extract
- 1 tablespoon spiced rum
- ½ cup cold heavy cream
- 2 tablespoons confectioners' sugar

- 2 cups broken shortbread cookies
- 3 large ripe bananas, sliced

DIRECTIONS:

1. Using a medium saucepan, stir together the egg yolks, granulated sugar, cornstarch, and salt over medium heat. Bring to a simmer and put in the milk while frequently stirring, 5 to 8 minutes. It starts bubbling, turns the heat down to low and continues cooking, constantly whisking, until the mixture thickens, which will take up to 2 minutes.
2. Put it away from the heat, and then add in the vanilla, canna-butter, and rum. Put the mixture to another bowl and place a piece of plastic wrap directly on the surface of the pudding to keep a film from forming. Refrigerate until set for a few hours.
3. Once the pudding is cold, place the cream in a bowl. Using a stand or electric mixer on medium-low speed, whip until the creamed well. Blend in the confectioners' sugar and whip until the cream holds silky, medium-firm peaks. Do not over mix
4. Into each of 6 parfait glasses, spoon a large dollop of the pudding mixture. Top with a layer of cookie pieces and a layer of sliced bananas. Do the same procedure and top it odd with the pudding. Crumble some of the cookie pieces and sprinkle over the top. Refrigerate until ready to serve.

Nutrition: Calories: 215, Fat:3g, Fiber: 1.4g, Carbs: 40.9, Protein: 0.9g

GET HIGH PUDDING

Preparation Time: 15 minutes - **Cooking Time:** 2 hrs. - **Servings:** 2

INGREDIENTS:

- 2cups dried figs soaked in 1/4 cup boiling water
- 1 cup of cannabis milk
- 1 1/2 cups all-purpose flour sifted
- 1 cup of sugar
- 2 1/2 teaspoons baking powder
- 1 tsp. pumpkin pie spice
- 1 teaspoon of sea salt
- 3 eggs
- 1/2 cup melted cannabis butter
- 1 1/2 cups breadcrumbs
- 1 tablespoon grated orange peel

DIRECTIONS:

1. Mix all ingredients until well blended. Pour into a greased bundt pan. Place into a water bath. Cover with nonstick foil loosely. Bake it until pudding is set and begins to release from the sides of the pan,

about 2 hrs.

Nutrition: Calories: 250, Fat:4,7g, Fiber: 1.4g, Carbs: 49g, Protein: 0.9g

MARIJUANA CREAMY CUSTARD

Preparation Time: 15 minutes - **Cooking Time:** 15-20 minutes - **Servings:** 2

INGREDIENTS:

- 1 spoon vanilla extract
- 3 eggs
- 0.3 to 0.5 marijuana flowers
- 600 grams of milk
- 90-130 grams of sugar

DIRECTIONS:

1. In a medium-sized bowl, combine the eggs and milk Add vanilla extract, dried buds and sugar Beat everything at medium speed Once the liquid has formed, continue mixing the batter for an extra two minutes Transfer the contents into a container and then let it set in the fridge Dust with cinnamon or top with fruits.

Nutrition: Calories: 208, Fat:1.4, Fiber: 1.9g, Carbs: 35g, Protein: 0.2g

"BAKED" PEACH PIE

Preparation Time: 15-20 minutes - **Cooking Time:** 50-60 minutes - **Servings:** 6-8

INGREDIENTS:

- ½ cup plus 2 tablespoons canna sugar
- ¼ cup packed brown sugar
- 5 cups fresh peaches peeled and sliced (see Note)
- 1 prepared pie shell or Canna Pie Crust
- 3 tablespoons potato starch or cornstarch
- 1 teaspoon cinnamon, divided
- ½ teaspoon ground cloves
- ¼ teaspoons salt
- 1 tablespoon cannabutter
- 2 teaspoons lemon juice
- 3 tablespoons heavy cream

Canna Pie Crust:

- 3 cups all-purpose flour

- 14 tablespoons cold butter, cubed
- 2 tablespoons granulated sugar
- 2 tablespoons cannabutter, cold
- 1½ teaspoons salt
- ½ cup plus 2 teaspoons ice-cold water

DIRECTIONS:

1. Preheat the oven to 400°F. In a large bowl, combine ½ cup of the CBD sugar and the brown sugar, add the peaches, and toss to coat. Cover and let stand for 1 hour. Roll out half of the chilled pie dough and lay it in the bottom of a 9-inch pie pan. Trim the edges, leaving about ½ inch of crust overhang. Drain the peaches, reserving the juice. In a small saucepan, combine the potato starch, ½ teaspoon of the cinnamon, the cloves, and CBD salt, and slowly add in the reserved peach juice and stir. Put the pan over medium heat, and bring to a boil. Cook for 2 minutes or until thickened. Remove it from the heat and stir in the CBD butter and lemon juice. Pour the mixture over the peaches, carefully fold in, and then pour the filling into the crust. Roll out the remaining pastry and make a lattice or your favorite top crust. Trim, seal, and flute the edges. Mix together the remaining ½ teaspoon of cinnamon and 2 tablespoons CBD sugar. Brush the top of the uncooked pie crust with the cream and sprinkle with the cinnamon-sugar mixture. Cover the edges with foil, so they don't bake too quickly, and bake for 50 to 60 minutes, or until the filling is bubbly and the crust is golden.
2. Canna Pie Crust:
3. Mix together all the ingredients except water in the food processor. Pulse 4 to 5 times, then add the water, processing just until the dough comes together—you still want to see pea-size pieces of butter. Divide the dough into two equal pieces, wrap in plastic, and refrigerate for at least 1 hour or until ready to use.

Nutrition: Calories: 289, Fat:8.9g, Fiber: 2.8g, Carbs: 52.1, Protein: 0.9g

FRESH GLAZED VERY RED BERRY PIE

Preparation Time: 1 hr. **- Cooking Time:** 10-15 minutes **- Servings:** 3-4

INGREDIENTS:

- ½ cup regular sugar
- ½ cup canna sugar
- 1 pkg. Jell-O Raspberry Jelly Powder
- 2 tablespoon corn starch
- 1 cup of water
- 1 baked (9-inch) pie shell, cooled
- 3 cups fresh strawberries, hulled

- 2 cups fresh raspberries
- 1 cup heavy cream, whipped

DIRECTIONS:

1. Mix sugar, dry jelly powder and corn starch in a medium saucepan. Gradually Blend in water. Then let it boil under medium-high heat while whisking continuously. Cook and stir until thickened. Let cool 10 min. Fill pie shell with berries; cover with jelly glaze. Refrigerate 1 hour. Top with whipped cream before serving.

Nutrition: Calories: 265, Fat:5.4g, Fiber: 1.4g, Carbs: 67.1g, Protein: 1.2g

BLUEBERRY-PEACH COBBLER

Preparation Time: 20 minutes   **- Cooking Time:** 45-50 minutes **- Servings:** 8

INGREDIENTS:

- ¼ cup (4 tablespoons/½ stick) unsalted butter, melted, plus more for the pan
- 4 cups sliced peeled peaches
- 1-pint blueberries (about 4 cups)
- 1 tablespoon cornstarch
- 1 teaspoon ground cinnamon
- ½ teaspoon ground ginger
- ¾ cup granulated sugar
- 2 tablespoons plus 2 teaspoons Canna sugar
- 1 cup all-purpose flour
- 2 teaspoons baking powder
- ⅛ teaspoon freshly grated nutmeg
- ⅛ teaspoon salt
- 1 cup whole milk Whipped cream, vanilla ice cream, or crème fraîche, for serving

DIRECTIONS:

1. Preheat the oven to 350°F. Lightly butter a 3-quart baking dish. In a bowl, mix together the melted butter, peaches, blueberries, cornstarch, cinnamon, ginger, and ¼ cup of the granulated sugar. Ina medium bowl, whisk together the remaining½ cup granulated sugar, canna sugar, flour, baking powder, nutmeg, and salt. Slowly whisk in the milk. Pour the batter into the prepared baking dish and top with the fruit mixture. Next, bake it until it is golden in color the filling is bubbling and thick around the edges, maybe around 45 minutes, serve hot from the oven topped with whipped cream, vanilla ice cream, or crème fraîche. Cover and refrigerate any leftover cobbler for up to 4 days.

Nutrition: Calories: 255, Fat:6g, Fiber: 2.4g, Carbs: 50.1, Protein: 0.4g

CHOCOLATE CITRUS TORTE

Preparation Time: 15 minutes plus cooling time **- Cooking Time:** 10-15 minutes **- Servings:** 4-6

INGREDIENTS:

- 1 canna pie crust
- 8 ounces dark chocolate, chopped fine
- 6 tablespoons butter, unsalted, cut in a piece
- 1 Canna Spicy Jelly Spice Blend
- 2 tablespoons orange zest
- 2 tablespoons grapefruit zest
- ¼ cup boiling water
- 1 egg yolk
- Whipped Cream for topping

DIRECTIONS:

1. Over a double boiler, melt on low chocolate, butter, orange zest, grapefruit zest. Then, Whisk for 3 minutes in a double boiler over low heat. Strain out the egg yolk and mix well with chocolate. Pour into cooled crust and chill. Top with Whip Cream.

Nutrition: Calories: 245, Fat:4.1g, Fiber: 3.4g, Carbs: 49.1, Protein: 0.10g

LEMON RASPBERRY SCONES

Preparation Time: 35-40 minutes **- Cooking Time:** 15-20 minutes **- Servings:** 8-10

INGREDIENTS:

- Scones
- 2-3 cups cake flour
- 2 tsp. baking powder
- 1/4 cup sugar
- 1/2 teaspoon ground cardamom
- 1 tablespoon lemon zest (zest of 1 lemon)
- 5 tablespoons cold canna-butter, cut into chunks
- 1 cup heavy cream, plus more for brushing before baking
- 1 cup frozen raspberry
- 1/2 teaspoon salt
- Glaze
- 1/3 cup lemon juice

- 2 1/2 cups confectioners' sugar
- 2 tablespoons heavy cream

DIRECTIONS:

1. Bring the temperature of your oven to 400 F. with a piece of parchment paper, line a baking sheet
2. Place salt, flour, sugar, baking powder, cardamom, and lemon zest in the bowl of a food processor and pulse one or two times to mix. Add cold cannabis-infused butter and pulse a few times until the mixture forms coarse crumbs. Blend in the cream and pulse a few times just until incorporated. Remove dough from food processor and place in a large bowl. Fold in berries. Gather dough into a disc, wrap in plastic wrap, and refrigerate for at least 30 minutes. To cut in butter and dry ingredients using a dough scraper, then mix in cream by hand before folding in berries.
3. Roll dough to about 1/2-inch thickness on a lightly floured surface. Use a three 1/2-inch round cutter to cut out circles. Place on the prepared baking sheet. The scones must be brushed with butter or cream and bake for about 15 minutes or until tops are lightly browned. Let cool completely before applying the glaze.
4. Prepare glaze by mixing lemon juice, confectioners' sugar and heavy cream until smooth. Pour glaze over cooled scones.
5. Freezer Friendly!
   Wrap fresh baked glazed scones individually in plastic wrap, place in a plastic freezer bag, and freeze. Bring to room temperature and enjoy.

Nutrition: Calories: 241, Fat:2.9g, Fiber: 4g, Carbs: 56g, Protein: 0.81g

CHOCOLATE COCONUT PECAN PIE

Preparation Time: 15-20 minutes - **Cooking Time:** 30 minutes - **Servings:** 8-10

INGREDIENTS:

- ¼ cup melted cannabutter
- ¾ cup of sugar
- 2¼ teaspoons vanilla extract
- 3 eggs slightly beaten
- 3 tablespoons all-purpose flour
- 6 ounces sweetened dark
- chocolate bar, finely chopped
- ½ cup chopped pecans
- ½ cup shredded unsweetened
- coconut
- 9-inch prepared piecrust

- Whipped cream for topping

DIRECTIONS:

1. Preheat your oven to 350°.In a bowl, put in sugar, melted cannabutter, and vanilla extract. Mix it well, and then add in the flour and the eggs gradually...Ensure it is combined thoroughly. Fold in the pecan nuts, chocolate and coconut. Next, pour the mixture into the prepared piecrust and bake for around 30 minutes. The pie will rise during baking. After baking, let it cool in a rack, and when done, serve it with whipped cream on top.

Nutrition: Calories: 221, Fat:5.6g, Fiber: 1.4g, Carbs: 41.7, Protein: 0.76g

STONED GUMMIES

Preparation Time: 15-20 minutes **- Cooking Time:** 5 minutes **- Servings:** 30 pcs

INGREDIENTS:

- Nonstick cooking spray
- 1 large packet (6 ounces) Jell-O, your preferred flavor
- Four ¼-ounce envelopes unflavored gelatin
- ½ cup of cold water
- ¼ cup Cannabis Tincture
- Cornstarch, for dusting
- Special equipment: silicone gummy molds, funnel or dropper

DIRECTIONS:

1. Grease the molds lightly with the cooking spray, then wipe with a paper towel, so very little oil remains. Place the molds on a rimmed baking sheet. In a small saucepan, whisk the Jell-O and gelatin together, then add the cold water and whisk to combine. Over medium heat, bring Jell-O mixture to a boil, then reduce heat to low and cook for 5 minutes, stirring often. Remove it from heat and let cool slightly. Add the tincture and mix well. Using a funnel or dropper, fill the molds. Place the baking sheet in the fridge and let chill for 15 minutes. Pop the gummies out of the molds and dust lightly with cornstarch to prevent sticking. Prolong its shelf life by Storing them in a glass container in the fridge.

Nutrition: Calories: 128, Fat:2.7g, Fiber: 1g, Carbs: 29.9g, Protein: 0.4g

GANJA TOFFEE CHEWS

Preparation Time: 15- minutes **- Cooking Time:** 15 minutes **- Servings:** 24, pcs.

INGREDIENTS:

- 2 packs of saltine crackers

- 8 ounces of cannabutter
- 1 cup dark brown sugar
- 2 cups some flavor of confection chips semi-sweet, raspberry chocolate etc.
- 3/4 cup chopped nuts of your choice, depending on your flavor of chips.

DIRECTIONS:

1. First, line a half-size baking pan with 1 inch's sides with foil. Use a cooking spray to grease the foil and evenly distribute it, in a single layer, the saltine crackers, so they are covering the bottom of the pan but not overlapping. Also, preheat the oven to 350° and make sure the rack is in the center position. Into a heavy-bottomed saucepan, add the medicated butter and the sugar. When the mixture is already boiling, time it for exactly 3 minutes and then remove from the heat.

2. Quickly pour the molten mixture over the saltines and spread to cover crackers completely. Bake in the oven for 10 minutes. Remove the pan from the oven and expect that during the baking process, the mixture bubbled and probably put the crackers in wonky positions, but that's okay. Just poke them around with a fork to realign them. When they straighten out, pour the morsels over the candy and let it rest for a few minutes while it melts. Spread the melted morsels over the entire pan and top with chopped nuts. Let cool, or if you are in a hurry, stick them in the freezer for a while! I keep individual medicated pieces wrapped and frozen. They are excellent on ice cream or alone.

Nutrition: Calories: 134, Fat:2.1g, Fiber: 3g, Carbs: 47.6g, Protein: 0.7g

KIRSCH CHOCOLATE MUFFINS

Preparation Time: 15 minutes - **Cooking Time:** 20-25 minutes - **Servings:** 6-8

INGREDIENTS:

- 1/2 tsp. baking soda
- 1/2 cup of cannabutter
- ½ cup of roughly cut dark chocolate
- 3/4 cup of brown sugar
- 1/4 cup of either unsweetened cocoa powder (Dutch cocoa works too)
- 3/4 cup of milk
- 1 1/4 cups of self-rising flour
- 2 eggs
- 15 ounces of dark cherries in syrup (thawed, drained, whatever the preference)
- 1 tbsp. cocoa
- Extra 1 tsp. icing sugar

DIRECTIONS:

1. Set the oven to 350°F. Prepare a 12-hole muffin tray with liners. Cream the butter and sugar

together, adding a single egg at a time. Take the baking soda, the cocoa, and the flour and sift together with the butter mix from before. Finish up by combining with the milk, chocolate, and cherries. Try to fill each cupcake tin to approximately ¾ full and place in the preheated oven for 20-25 minutes. A sign that cupcakes are done is by doing the clean toothpick test. Once it is cooked, put it away from heat and let cool while the icing is made. Frost and enjoy it!

Nutrition: Calories: 196, Fat:4.2g, Fiber: 1.8, Carbs: 30.6g, Protein: 1.1g

CANNA- BANANA CRUMBLE MUFFINS

Preparation Time: 10-15 minutes **- Cooking Time:** 18-20 minutes **- Servings:** 8-10

INGREDIENTS:

- 1 ½ cups flour
- 1/3 cup cannabis butter
- 3 mashed bananas
- 3/4 cup cane sugar
- 1/3 cup packed brown sugar
- 1 tsp. baking soda
- 1 tsp. baking powder
- 1/2 tsp. table salt
- 1 egg
- 2 tbsp. flour
- 1 tbsp. butter
- 1/8 tsp. ground cinnamon

DIRECTIONS:

1. Bring the heat of your oven to 350 f. and lightly butter a 10-cup muffin tray. Get out a large mixing bowl and mix the 1.5 cups flour, baking soda, baking powder and salt. In a separate bowl, mix the mashed bananas, egg, cane sugar and 1/3 cup melted cannabis butter. Stir this mixture into the first mixture until just blended. Spread this batter evenly into the greased or buttered muffin cups. In another bowl, combine the brown sugar, cinnamon and 2 tbsp. Flour. Cut in 1 tbsp. Butter. Sprinkle this mixture over the muffin batter in the trays. Bake 18 - 20 minutes; allow cooling on a wire rack and enjoying.

Nutrition: Calories: 210, Fat:6g, Fiber: 2.4, Carbs: 35g, Protein: 1.7 g

LEMON COCONUT MUFFINS

Preparation Time: 10-15 minutes **- Cooking Time:** 15-20 minutes **- Servings:** 8-10

INGREDIENTS:

- 1 1/4 cup almond flour
- 1 cup shredded unsweetened coconut
- 2 tbsp. coconut flour
- 1/2 tsp. baking soda
- 1/2 tsp. baking powder
- 1/4 tsp. salt
- 1/4 cup of honey (raw)
- Juice and zest from 1 lemon
- 1/4 cup full-fat coconut milk
- 3 eggs, whisked
- 3 tbsp. medicated coconut oil
- 1 tsp. vanilla extract

DIRECTIONS:

1. Bring the heat of your oven to 350 f. In a small bowl, mix all the wet ingredients together. In a medium bowl, combine all the dry ingredients. Now pour the wet ingredients into the dry ingredients bowl and stir into a batter. Let your batter sit for a few minutes then stir it again. Now grease a muffin tin and fill each about two-thirds of the way full. Pop it in the oven and bake for about 20 minutes. Test the doneness of the muffin by inserting a toothpick in the center, and if it comes out clean, that means you are good to go. Remove from oven, let cool for a cool minute and serve!

Nutrition: Calories: 296, Fat:7,5g, Fiber: 3.2, Carbs: 50g, Protein: 1.9g

MARIJUANA OATMEAL BARS

Preparation Time: 15 minutes - **Cooking Time:** 25-30 minutes - **Servings:** 14-16

INGREDIENTS:

- 1¼ cups old-fashioned rolled oats
- 1¼ cups all-purpose flour
- ½ cup finely chopped toasted walnuts (see Note)
- ½ cup of sugar
- ½ teaspoon baking soda
- ¼ teaspoon salt
- 1 cup cannabutter, melted
- 2 teaspoons vanilla
- 1 cup good-quality jam
- 4 whole graham crackers (8 squares), crushed

- Whipped cream, for serving (optional)

DIRECTIONS:

1. Preheat the oven to 350°F. Grease a 9-inch square baking pan. In a bowl, put in and combine oatmeal, flour, walnuts, sugar, baking soda, and salt. In a small bowl, combine the butter and vanilla. Add the butter mixture to the oat mixture and mix until crumbly. Reserve 1 cup for topping, and press the remaining oat mixture into the bottom of the baking pan. Spread the jam evenly over the top. Add the crushed crackers to the reserved oat mixture and sprinkle over the jam. Bake it for around 25 to 30 minutes, or until the edges are browned. Cool completely in the pan on a rack. Cut into 16 squares. Serve, adding a dollop of whipped cream if desired. Storing it in a glass container in the fridge will help preserve it.

Nutrition: Calories: 299, Fat:6.8g, Fiber: 4.1, Carbs: 67g, Protein: 3.1

JANE'S CHEWY PECAN BARS

Preparation Time: 20 minutes - **Cooking Time:** 1 hr. and 15 minutes

INGREDIENTS:

- Nonstick baking spray
- 2 cups plus
- 2 tablespoons all-purpose flour, divided
- ½ cup granulated sugar
- 2 tablespoons plus
- 2 tsp. cannabutter
- 3½ teaspoons unsalted butter, cut into pieces
- ¾ teaspoon plus kosher pinch salt, divided
- ¾ cup packed dark brown sugar
- 4 large eggs
- 2 teaspoons vanilla extract
- 1 cup light corn syrup
- 2 cups chopped pecans
- Pecan nuts cut in half

DIRECTIONS:

1. Preheat the oven to 340°F. Grease the pan using a nonstick spray and line with parchment paper with an overhang on two sides so you can easily lift the bars from the pan. (The filling is sticky and can make it hard to remove without the parchment.)

2. By utilizing a blender or food processor, pulse flour, the sugar, kinds of butter, and ¾ teaspoon of salt until combined. The mixture will form into clumps. Transfer the dough to the prepared pan.

Press it firmly and evenly in the bottom of the pan. Pierce the crust all over with a fork and bake until light to a medium golden brown, 30 to 35 minutes.

3. Using the same food processor bowl, combine the brown sugar, the remaining 2 tablespoons flour, pinch salt, eggs, vanilla, and corn syrup. (Add the corn syrup last, so it doesn't get stuck on the bottom of the food processor.) Pulse until completely combined. Turn the mixture into a large bowl and add the pecans. Spoon the pecan mixture evenly over the baked crust. Place a few extra pecan halves on the top of the filling as decoration.

4. Place the pan back into the oven and let it bake until the center is just set 35 to 40 minutes. On the off chance that the inside still wiggles, prepare for a couple of more minutes; if you notice the bars are beginning to puff in the center, remove them right away. Put them in a rack and leave to cool before cutting into 16 (2-inch) squares and lifting the bars out.

5. Storage: Keep the bars in an airtight container at room temperature for 3 to 5 days or freeze for up to 6 months. They can be very sticky, so wrap them in parchment or wax paper.

Nutrition: Calories: 190, Fat:1.5g, Fiber: 4.1, Carbs: 26g, Protein: 1g

ORANGE CREAMSICLE COOKIES

Preparation Time: 10 minutes - **Cooking Time:** 10-15 minutes - **Servings:** 24 pcs

INGREDIENTS:

- 14 tablespoons (1¾ sticks) unsalted butter, softened
- 2 tablespoons cannabutter, softened
- ½ cup granulated sugar
- ½ cup packed light brown sugar
- 1 large egg, at room temperature
- 1½ tablespoons orange juice
- 2¼ cups all-purpose flour
- 2 tablespoons grated orange zest
- 1 teaspoon baking soda
- ½ teaspoon salt
- 2 cups white chocolate chips

DIRECTIONS:

1. Preheat the oven to 340°F. Put parchment paper on the baking sheet. By utilizing an electric mixer or stand mixer on medium speed, beat the kinds of butter and both sugars together for about 2 minutes. Add the egg and orange juice and mix for 30 seconds. Add the flour, zest, baking soda, and salt, and mix on low speed, increasing to medium-low speed, until the dough comes together. Stir in the chocolate chips until incorporated. Drop heaping 2-tablespoon scoops of the dough 2 inches apart

onto the prepared baking sheets. Bake the cookies until lightly golden, which may take about 8 to 10 minutes. Let cool for 3 minutes on the baking sheet, and then transfer the cookies to a wire rack to finish cooling.

2. Storage: Keep the cookies in an airtight container for 4 to 5 days or freeze for up to 6 months.

Nutrition: Calories: 275, Fat:2g, Fiber: 4.1, Carbs: 26.4g, Protein: 1.6g

CARAMEL CRUNCH BARS

INGREDIENTS:

- 1½ cups rolled oats
- 1½ cups flour
- ¾ cup brown sugar
- ½ teaspoon baking soda
- ¼ teaspoon salt
- ¼ cup melted cannabutter
- ¼ cup melted butter

Toppings

- ½ cup brown sugar
- ½ cup granulated sugar
- ½ cup butter
- ¼ cup flour
- 1 cup chopped nuts
- 1 cup chopped chocolate

DIRECTIONS:

1. Bring the temperature of your oven to 350 F. Put oats, flour, salt, sugar and baking soda in a bowl then mix well. Put in your cannabutter and the regular butter and mix until it forms crumbs. Put aside at least a cup of these crumbs for garnish later. Now prepare the pan by greasing it with a spray then put the oat mixture on the bottom part of the pan. Put it in the oven and bake for a while, then remove it once it is quite brown then let it cool. Then next is to make the caramel. Do this by stirring the butter and sugar in a saucepan that has a thick bottom to avoid it from burning quickly. Allow it bubble then after adding in the flour. Back to the oatmeal base, add the mixed nuts and chocolate followed by the caramel you just made, and then lastly, top it off with the extra crumbs you set aside. Place it back in the oven and let it cook until the bars are golden in color, which will take for about 20 minutes. After baking, cool it down before you cut into whatever size you want.

Nutrition: Calories: 196, Fat:2.8g, Fiber: 3g, Carbs: 31g, Protein: 1.8 g

MARIJUANA SNOWBALLS

Preparation Time: 1 ½ hr. **- Cooking Time:** 20-25 minutes **- Servings:** 12

INGREDIENTS:

- 1 cup cannabutter, softened
- 1/4 cup sugar
- 1 tsp. pure vanilla extract
- 2 cups all-purpose flour
- 2 Tbsp. cornstarch
- 1 cup of unsalted roasted almonds, finely chopped
- 1/4 tsp. salt
- 1 cup of powdered sugar to coat

DIRECTIONS:

1. By utilizing a stand mixer or a hand mixer, beat the cannabutter with 1/4 cup of the sugar until creamy. Add the vanilla extract. Gently beat in the flour, corn starch, roasted almonds and salt until well combined. Wrap in plastic wrap and refrigerate for one hour. Preheat oven to 325°. Take the chilled dough out from the fridge and get about a tbsp. of dough then shape it into a 1-inch ball. Arrange the balls on the baking sheet about 1 inch apart. Bake the cookies on the middle shelf of the oven for 20 minutes, or until golden and set. Fill a shallow bowl with 1 cup of sifted powdered sugar. Cool for around 5 minutes, and when cool enough to touch, roll the cookies in the powdered sugar and set aside on the parchment-lined rack to cool completely. When cool, dust again in the powdered sugar and store in an airtight container.
2. Note: You can also use pecans, walnuts, hazelnuts, macadamia, almonds or any of your favorite nuts in place of the almonds or a combination as they all work well.

Nutrition: Calories: 215, Fat:5.8g, Fiber: 2g, Carbs: 41g, Protein: 0.7g

CITRUS POPPY SEED COOKIES

Preparation Time: 15 minutes **- Cooking Time:** 10-15 minutes **- Servings:** 36 pcs

INGREDIENTS:

- 1/2 tsp. of baking soda
- 1 tbsp. of orange zest
- 1 tsp. orange juice
- 1 tbsp. of poppy seeds
- 1/2 cup of cannabutter
- 2/3 cup of sugar

* 1 1/4 cup of flour
* 1 egg
* Dash of salt

DIRECTIONS:

1. Set the oven to 350°F for preheating. Whisk the sugar and cannabutter together for about 2 minutes. This will leave a light batter, relatively fluffy. Add the orange zest, the orange juice, and the egg, making sure to mix each one for best results thoroughly. Take another bowl and sift the baking soda, salt, and flour together. Add the sifted mixture to the original batter, and mix only long enough to see them combined before folding in the poppy seeds.
2. Tip: For chewier cookies, line the cookie sheets before baking. Parchment paper works best!
3. The mix is now ready to be placed onto the cookie sheets. Take a teaspoon and parcel out the pieces, making sure to leave even spaces between each cookie. Place in the oven and bake for about 10-12 minutes, the cookies are ultimately done when the edges are golden. Remove from the heat, let them cool down, and enjoy!

Nutrition: Calories: 216, Fat:6.1g, Fiber: 4.1, Carbs: 35g, Protein: 1g

GANJA GINGER COOKIES

Preparation Time: 35-40 minutes - **Cooking Time:** 8-10 minutes - **Servings:** 10-12

INGREDIENTS:

* 2 cups self-rising flour
* 2 tbsp. ground ginger powder
* ¾ tbsp. ground cinnamon
* ½ tbsp. ground cloves
* ¼ tsp. salt
* ¾ cup cannabutter
* 1 cup white sugar
* 1 egg
* 1 tbsp. water
* 4 tbsp. molasses

DIRECTIONS:

1. Preheat your oven to the temperature of 180c. Sift the ginger, flour, baking soda, cloves, cinnamon and salt together. Cream the butter with the sugar in a separate bowl and beat the egg in. Add the molasses and water, and stir to mix. Add the dry ingredients gradually, stirring to combine. Spoon the mix onto plastic wrap and roll into a sausage shape. Leave for about 30 minutes to harden off. Slice the roll into rounds about 1 inch thick and place them onto an ungreased sheet, about 2 inches

apart. Flatten each round a little. Back for about 8 to 10 minutes and then leave to cool for 5 minutes before transferring to a wire rack

Nutrition: Calories: 188, Fat:3.2g, Fiber: 2g, Carbs: 29,9g, Protein: 0.5g

CANNABIS OATMEAL COOKIES

Preparation Time: 10 minutes - **Cooking Time:** 20 minutes - **Servings:** 2

INGREDIENTS:

- 1/4 cup of cannabis butter
- 2 cups packed dark brown sugar
- 1 cup (2 sticks) salted butter, softened
- 2 teaspoons of vanilla extract
- 1 1/2 cups all-purpose flour
- 1 teaspoon of salt
- 1/2 teaspoon of baking soda
- 3 cups of old-fashioned oats

DIRECTIONS:

1. Preheat your oven to the temperature of 180c. Using a bowl, beat the brown sugar and both butter until fluffy. Beat in the vanilla. Gradually add the egg into the mixture then scrape the bowl after each bowl. Mix the flour, salt and baking soda in a medium bowl. Add it to the creamy mixture in 2 to 3 servings, mix until just combined. Mix the oats until just combined. Use your preferred cookie spoon (or a regular spoon) to drop portions of dough onto baking sheets, with spacing in between. Bake it for 12 to 13 minutes or until cookies are chewy and set.

Nutrition: Calories: 214, Fat:3g, Fiber: 2.1, Carbs: 43g, Protein: 0.9g

JAM THUMBPRINT COOKIES

Preparation Time: 15 minutes - **Cooking Time:** 15-20 minutes - **Servings:** 3-4

INGREDIENTS:

- 1 ¼ Cups all-purpose flour
- Dash Salt
- 1/3 Cup Pure Cane Sugar
- 4 tbsp. cannabutter melted
- ½ tsp. vanilla
- ¼ Cup milk (room temp)
- Peanut Butter and/or Jelly

* Any type of jam or nut butter

DIRECTIONS:

1. Preheat your oven to the temperature of 180c. Put parchment paper in a pan or cookie sheet and put aside. Combine flour, salt & sugar. Whisk! Add melted cannabutter, vanilla and milk. Mix and knead the dough until smooth. Pull 1" chunks off of the dough ball, and roll them into spheres. Place cookies on parchment paper and press center with your thumb. Fill thumb divot with Peanut Butter and Jelly. Bake until golden (about 15-20 minutes).

Nutrition: Calories: 150, Fat:2.1g, Fiber: 1g, Carbs: 28.5g, Protein: 0.7g

SUMMER STRAWBERRY COOKIES

Preparation Time: 15 minutes - **Cooking Time:** 10-12 minutes - **Servings:** 12

INGREDIENTS:

* ½ cup of canna Butter
* 1½ cups of flour
* ½ teaspoon of baking powder
* 1 package of strawberry gelatin
* 1 teaspoon of vanilla extract
* 1 egg

DIRECTIONS:

1. Preheat oven to 350° F. Cream the Baked Butter or margarine and gelatin in a bowl.
2. In another bowl, mix the baking powder, flour, egg, and vanilla extract together. Add this mixture to the cream of butter and gelatin; beat with an electric mixer for about 2 minutes.
3. Roll out the dough and cut it into square shapes. Place the cut cookies on a non-greased cookie sheet. Bake cookies in the oven for about 10 to 12 minutes. Let them cool. One to two cookies should do the trick.

Nutrition: Calories: 215, Fat:4g, Fiber: 1.4g, Carbs: 31g, Protein: 1.1g

ITALIAN MANDORLA COOKIES

Preparation Time: 15 minutes - **Cooking Time:** 12-15 minutes - **Servings:** 14-18

INGREDIENTS:

* 1/2 cup of cannabutter
* 1 cup of sugar
* 1 egg
* 1 teaspoon of almond extract

- 2 cups of all-purpose flour, sifted
- 1 teaspoon of baking powder
- 2 tablespoons of Marijuana Milk
- 1 cup of chopped almonds
- 1/3 cup of apricot jams

DIRECTIONS:

1. Cream the canna Butter, sugar, egg and almond extract together in a large mixing bowl. Add the flour, baking powder and milk then blend together well. Roll small amounts of dough for each cookie. Roll each ball between your palms like you would for peanut butter cookies or even meatballs. Roll the balls in the chopped almonds and place them on greased cookie sheets. Make an indentation with your thumb or the back of a spoon and fill the dent with jam. Bake for 12 to 15 minutes. Two cookies should get you baked.

Nutrition: Calories: 177, Fat:3.1g, Fiber: .8g, Carbs: 30.5g, Protein: 1.2g

VERY BERRY CHEESECAKE POPS

Preparation Time: 10-15 minutes - **Cooking Time:** 0 minutes - **Servings:** 4

INGREDIENTS:

- 4 ounces low-fat cream cheese
- 3/4 cup plain yogurt
- 1/4 cup agave syrup
- 1 teaspoon lemon or lime juice
- 2 gram decarboxylated kief or finely ground decarboxylated hash
- 3/4 cup fresh raspberries
- 3/4 cup fresh blueberries

DIRECTIONS:

1. Make the cream cheese light and fluffy using a stand mixer or a hand mixer. Using the low speed, add in agave syrup, yogurt, lime or lemon juice until it combined well. Next, fold in the berries using a rubber spatula. Put the mixture into popsicle molds then put them in the freezer.

Nutrition: Calories: 200, Fat:5.9g, Fiber: 2.1, Carbs: 54.6g, Protein: 1.1g

MANGO YOGURT POPS

Preparation Time: 10 minutes - **Cooking Time:** 0 minutes - **Servings:** 4

INGREDIENTS:

- 3 tbsp. coconut sugar

- 2 mangoes, peeled and cut
- 3 tbsp. canna coconut oil
- 2 cups vanilla yogurt
- 2 tsp. coconut extract

DIRECTIONS:

1. Toss in all the ingredients in the blender. Puree until it forms a smooth mix. Transfer mix into Popsicle molds. Freeze molds.

Nutrition: Calories: 210, Fat:7g, Fiber: 2g, Carbs: 43g, Protein: 2.1g

NUTTY BANANA YOGURT POPS

Preparation Time: 10 minutes **- Cooking Time:** 0 minutes **- Servings:** 6

INGREDIENTS:

- 1½ cups vanilla yogurt
- ¼ cup unsweetened cocoa powder
- 1 tablespoon Canna-Coconut Oil
- 1 ripe medium banana, sliced and frozen
- 1 tablespoon honey
- ½ cup chopped peanuts

DIRECTIONS:

1. In a blender, purée the yogurt, cocoa, canna-coconut oil, banana, and honey until smooth. Put the blend into another bowl and mix in the peanuts. Pour the mixture into popsicle molds and freeze until firm. Remove the pops from the molds according to the manufacturer's instructions.
2. Storage: Keep the pops in an airtight container in the freezer for up to several months.

Nutrition: Calories: 180, Fat:1.5g, Fiber: 2.4g, Carbs: 28,9g, Protein: 0,6g

DOUBLE CHOCOLATE GELATO

Preparation Time: 15 -20 minutes **- Cooking Time:** 5 to 10 minutes **- Servings:** 4-6

INGREDIENTS:

- 1/2 cup heavy cream
- 2 cups of milk
- 3/4 cup sugar
- 1/4 teaspoon salt
- 7 ounces high-quality dark chocolate
- 1 teaspoon vanilla extract

- Cannabis butter

DIRECTIONS:

1. The first step is done by melting the chocolate, then cooling it for a bit. Place the milk, cream, and cannabis butter in a bowl and mix them together until well combined. Mix in the sugar by using a whisk and salt. Continue to whisk for about 4 minutes until the sugar and salt dissolve. Then mix in the vanilla extract. Finally, mix in the chocolate until well combined. Pour the ingredients into your ice cream maker, and let it churn for 25 minutes. Put the gelato in an airtight container and place in the freezer for up to 2 hours, until desired consistency is reached.

Nutrition: Calories: 230, Fat:9g, Fiber: g, Carbs: 60.1g, Protein: 4g

CANNA CHERRY-STRAWBERRY GELATO

Preparation Time: 20 minutes - **Cooking Time:** 0 minutes - **Servings:** 4-6

INGREDIENTS:

- 1/2 cup heavy cream
- 2 cups of milk
- 3/4 cup sugar
- Cannabis butter*
- 1 cup sliced strawberries
- 1 tablespoon vanilla extract

DIRECTIONS:

1. Using a blender, puree the strawberry thoroughly. Place the milk, cream, and cannabis butter in a bowl and mix them together until well combined. Mix in the sugar by using a whisk. Continue to whisk for about 4 minutes until the sugar dissolves. Then mix in the vanilla extract and strawberry puree. Pour the ingredients into your ice cream maker, and let it churn for 25 minutes. Put the gelato in an airtight container and place in the freezer for up to 2 hours, until desired consistency is reached.

Nutrition: Calories: 210, Fat:6.8g, Fiber: 6g, Carbs: 34.6g, Protein: 3g

PEACHES-N-CREAM SOFT SERVE ICE CREAM

Preparation Time: 35 minutes - **Cooking Time:** 0 minutes - **Servings:** 4-6

INGREDIENTS:

- 2 cups heavy cream

- 1 cup milk
- 3⁄4 cup sugar
- Cannabis butter
- 1 Tbs. vanilla extract
- 1 cup sliced peaches

DIRECTIONS:

1. Using a blender, puree the peaches thoroughly. Place the milk, cream, and cannabis butter in a bowl and mix them together until well combined. Mix in the sugar by using a whisk. Continue to whisk for about 4 minutes until the sugar dissolves. Then mix in the vanilla extract. Then mix in the peaches. Put all the prepared ingredients in a clean ice cream maker and let it churn for 25 minutes. Serve immediately.

Nutrition: Calories: 240, Fat:6g, Fiber: 2g, Carbs: 56g, Protein: 1.5g

TROPICAL MANGO SOFT SERVE ICE CREAM

Preparation Time: 35 minutes - **Cooking Time:** 0 minutes - **Servings:** 6

INGREDIENTS:

- 2 cups heavy cream
- 1 cup milk
- 3⁄4 cup sugar
- 1 Tbs. vanilla extract
- 1 cup pureed mango (about 2.5 mangos)
- Juice of 1 lime
- Cannabis butter

DIRECTIONS:

1. Puree the mangos with the lime juice in a food processor or blender.
2. Place the milk, cream, and cannabis butter in a bowl and mix them together until well combined. Use a whisk to mix in the sugar. Continue to whisk for about 4 minutes until the sugar dissolves. Then mix in the vanilla extract. Then mix in the mango puree.
3. Put all the prepared ingredients in a clean ice cream maker and let it churn for 25 minutes.
4. Serve immediately.

Nutrition: Calories: 176, Fat:2.1g, Fiber: 6g, Carbs: 36g, Protein: 0.4g

LIME COCONUT ICE POPS

Preparation Time: 10 minutes **- Cooking Time:** 0 minutes **- Servings:** 4

INGREDIENTS:

- 1 14 ounces canna coconut milk, canned
- 1 cup cream
- 2 tablespoons limeade concentrate
- 1 tablespoon lime zest
- 2 tablespoons lemon juice
- Pinch of salt

DIRECTIONS:

1. Toss in all the ingredients in the blender. Puree until it forms a smooth mix. Transfer mix into Popsicle molds. Freeze molds.

Nutrition: Calories: 180, Fat:2.5g, Fiber: 8g, Carbs: 35.9g, Protein: 0.2g

ROSE COCONUT ICE CREAM

INGREDIENTS:

- ⅓ cup Rose Tea
- 2 ¾ cup canna cream
- 10 egg yolks
- 5 tablespoons Simple Syrup
- 1 cup coconut, shredded

DIRECTIONS:

1. In a double boiler heat until nearly boiling and remove from the heat rose tea and cream. In a separate bowl, whisk until frothy eggs and milk. Pour the warm milk over the eggs whisking continually, then back into the pan over low heat. Cook and stir until the mixture thickens.
2. The mixture must be strained to a clean bowl and add coconut. Cover with plastic wrap and cool at room temperature. Pour into an electric ice cream machine and follow the manufactures direction.

Nutrition: Calories: 190, Fat:3.2, Fiber: 3g, Carbs: 45g, Protein: 0.6g

CHAI GREEN TEA ICE CREAM

Preparation Time: 15 minutes **- Cooking Time:** 10-15 minutes **- Servings:** 4-6

INGREDIENTS:

- 2 cups heavy cream

- 2 Chai Tea Blend, dry
- 6 egg yolks
- 1 cup of the warm cream
- ¼ cup instant coffee granular
- 3 tablespoons stevia
- 3 tablespoons canna sugar
- 2 teaspoons vanilla
- ½ cup Chai Tea

DIRECTIONS:

1. Mix everything in under a double boiler and heat up gradually. Once the mixture is smooth and kind of thick, remove from heat and cool down. After this, put in the ice cream maker and churn. Transfer to a container and freeze.

Nutrition: Calories: 199, Fat:5g, Fiber: 2g, Carbs: 45g, Protein: 0.9g

INDIAN SWEET CARROT PUDDING

Preparation Time: 25 minutes - **Cooking Time:** 30 minutes - **Servings:** 4

INGREDIENTS:

- 5 large carrots shredded
- 1 cup milk
- ½ cup sweetened condensed milk
- ½ cup turbinado sugar
- ½ cup raisins
- ¼ cup raw cashews
- 4 tablespoons Cannabutter
- 1 teaspoon cardamom powder

DIRECTIONS:

1. Place the Cannabutter, raisins and cashews into a frying pan. Sauté this mixture on medium-high for 3 minutes while constantly stirring. Immediately reduce the heat to medium and add in the shredded carrots. Add in the milk, condensed milk and simmer this mixture on medium for 10 minutes while occasionally stirring to break up any clumps. After 10 minutes of simmering, stir in the sugar and continue to cook this mixture in the same setting until the liquid is absorbed by the carrots. This process of allowing the carrots to absorb the liquid will take approximately 15 minutes. Make sure you stir the mixture while it cooks to prevent the mixture from over caramelizing. After the liquid is absorbed, pull from heat and stir in the cardamom powder. Serve this dessert warm from the pan with vanilla ice cream on top or serve it chilled by itself. The plate then serves it by pouring the

mixture into a small bowl or large ramekin and allowing it to cool and set to that shape, then turning it out onto a plate. Indian Kalichakra Sweet Carrot Pudding can be stored in the refrigerator for up to 1 week.

Nutrition: Calories: 250, Fat:4g, Fiber: 1.2g, Carbs: 46g, Protein: 1.4g

JUANITA'S CANNA LOLLIPOP

Preparation Time: 5 minutes **- Cooking Time:** 20 minutes **- Servings:** 2

INGREDIENTS:

- 1 tbsp. cannabis tincture
- 1 cup of sugar
- 1/2 cup light corn syrup
- 1/4 cup of water
- 1 teaspoon of lemon extract or other flavors

DIRECTIONS:

1. In a medium saucepan, add sugar, light corn syrup, 1/4 cup of water. Slowly heat your pan until you reach 300F while beating the whole process. Remove from the fire. Add your extract and cannabis tincture. Beat well so that your tincture is distributed in the mixture. Set up your lollipop shape and lollipop sticks. Pour the blend prepared molds and allow them to cool.

Nutrition: Calories: 125, Fat:2.1g, Fiber: 1g, Carbs: 29.4g, Protein: 0.2g

CANNA MINT PATTIES

Preparation Time: 15 minutes to 4 hrs. for cooling **- Cooking Time:** 0 minutes **- Servings:** 24 pcs

INGREDIENTS:

- ½ cup of light corn syrup
- 2 teaspoon of peppermint extract
- ½ cup of softened cannabutter
- 2 drops of food coloring (optional)
- 9 cups of sifted powdered sugar (about 2 pounds)

DIRECTIONS:

1. Use a mixing bowl to mix the corn syrup, peppermint extract, and slightly melted Baked Butter or margarine. Then add the sugar, a little bit at a time, and incorporate it into the mix. Add the amount of food coloring to achieve your desired color and blend well.

2. Roll this mixture into small balls. Place them a few inches apart from each other on a baking sheet that has been lined with wax paper. Use a fork to make each one flat.

3. Let the mint patties set in the refrigerator for several hours. Remove the patties from the refrigerator and let stand at room temperature for several days to dry out. After a few days, when the patties are dried out, transfer them to a container with an airtight lid and store them in the refrigerator. You'll make about 24 patties. Eat 3 to 4 patties per (regular size) person to get baked.

Nutrition: Calories: 140, Fat:2.g, Fiber: 1.7g, Carbs: 41g, Protein: 0.9g

TROPICAL ORANGE CHEWS

Preparation Time: 20 minutes - **Cooking Time:** 25-30 minutes - **Servings:** 24 pcs

INGREDIENTS:

- ½ cup of cannabutter
- 2 cups of brown sugar
- 2 slightly beaten eggs
- 2 teaspoons of vanilla
- 3 teaspoons of freshly grated orange rind
- 1 cup of flour
- 1 teaspoon of salt
- 2 teaspoons of baking powder
- 2 cups of shredded coconut
- 2 cups of chopped dates

DIRECTIONS:

1. Preheat oven to 350° F. Grease a 9 by 9-inch pan.
2. In a saucepan, melt the Baked Butter or margarine then remove the saucepan from the heat. Stir in the brown sugar, vanilla, and orange rind. Once those ingredients are well combined, add the eggs. In a bowl or on a piece of waxed paper, combine the dry ingredients. Make sure to sift the dry ingredient at least three times. Mix the wet and dry ingredients together until completely mixed. Pour the batter into a prepared baking dish. Bake for 25 to 30 minutes. Cut into 16 squares when thoroughly cooled. If you like, roll each square into a ball and roll in more coconut. One to one and a half pieces/squares/balls will get you baked.

Nutrition: Calories: 130, Fat:2.7g, Fiber: 1g, Carbs: 31g, Protein: 0.3g

PEANUT BUTTER CUPS

Preparation Time: 1 hr. or overnight - **Cooking Time:** 0 minutes - **Servings:** 24 cups

INGREDIENTS:

- 1 cup unsalted toasted almonds

- 1 cup pitted dates
- 2 tablespoons cocoa powder
- 1 tablespoon cannabutter
- ½ cup peanut or cashew butter
- 1 tablespoon almond flour
- 1 cup semisweet chocolate chips, melted
- 2 tablespoons canna oil
- ½ teaspoon almond extract
- 1 teaspoon vanilla extract
- Sparkling sugar, for finishing

DIRECTIONS:

1. Prepare your muffin tray by putting liners on it. By the utilization of a blender or food processor, blend together dates, almonds cocoa powder, and CBD butter and pulse until it holds together. Press about 1 tablespoon of the almond mixture into the bottom of each cupcake liner. In a small bowl, combine the peanut butter and almond flour. Spread about 1 teaspoon of the peanut butter mixture on top of each cup. Put the tray in the chiller until the peanut mixture is firm. Meanwhile, in a small bowl, mix the chocolate chips, oil, and extracts. Remove the tin from the freezer and carefully spoon about 1½ teaspoons of the chocolate over each cup and smooth to the edges. Sprinkle with the sparkling sugar, freeze until firm, and enjoy.

Nutrition: Calories: 135, Fat:2.5g, Fiber: 1.4g, Carbs: 31.5g, Protein: 0.3g

CHOCOLATE COVERED CHERRIES

Preparation Time: 1 ½ hr. **- Cooking Time:** 5 minutes **- Servings:** 12

INGREDIENTS:

- 24 cherries with stems (remove the pits or use dried ones)
- 1 cup milk chocolate chips
- 1 cup dark chocolate chips
- ¼ cup of cannabis coconut oil

DIRECTIONS:

1. In a microwave-safe bowl, heat dark chocolate chips, milk chocolate chips and cannabis coconut oil. Heat the mix for 20-seconds intervals and stir by turns until it has finally melted. Ensure the chocolate is not too hot. Cover the cherries with chocolate, and let the excess chocolate drip. Set the cherries onto a wax-lined paper. Once all the cherries are done, transfer them into the refrigerator for 1-hour Double coat the cherries if you want (transfer into the refrigerator again) Enjoy!

Nutrition: Calories: 210, Fat:4g, Fiber: 2.1g, Carbs: 35g, Protein: 0.8g

CANNA CHOCOLATE TRUFFLES

Preparation Time: 15-20 minutes - **Cooking Time:** 0 minutes - **Servings:** 10-12

INGREDIENTS:

- ½ cup cannabutter softened
- ½cup powdered sugar
- ¼cup unsweetened cocoa powder
- ½cup almond flour
- Large pinch salt
- Dash almond extract
- Dash vanilla extract
- 24whole almonds, toasted in cannabutter and Salt
- 1cup unsweetened shredded coconut

DIRECTIONS:

1. Line a baking sheet with parchment paper. In a bowl, put all the prepared ingredients except the whole almonds and coconut and mix gently until the mixture is fairly smooth. Roll teaspoons of the mixture between your palms into balls. (Work quickly, as the butter gets very soft quickly. Refrigerate for a few minutes if the mixture gets too soft.) If using the toasted almonds, tuck one into the center of each and roll again quickly to smooth things over. Place the coconut in a bowl and roll the balls in the coconut until coated. Place on the baking sheet and refrigerate to firm up. Store the munchies in a glass container in the fridge.

Nutrition: Calories: 141, Fat:2.1g, Fiber: 1.4g, Carbs: 31.5g, Protein: 0.2g

MARIJUANA FUDGE MUNCHIES

Preparation Time: 10 minutes - **Cooking Time:** 0 minutes - **Servings:** 6-8

INGREDIENTS:

- 1/2 Cup cannabutter
- 1/2 Cup Almond Butter
- 1/8 to 1/4 cup Honey
- 1/2 of a Banana, Mashed
- 1 tsp. Vanilla Extract
- any kind of nut butter
- 1/8 Cup Dried Fruit
- 1/8 Cup Chocolate Chips

DIRECTIONS:

1. In a blender or food processer, add in all the ingredients. Blend for several minutes until smooth.
2. Pour the batter into a loaf pan with the lining of baking paper. For larger chunks, use a mini loaf pan or double the recipe. Refrigerate or freeze until firm. Cut into 8 equal squares.

Nutrition: Calories: 210, Fat:2.9g, Fiber: 1.7g, Carbs: 31.9g, Protein: 0.4g

OAT MUNCHIES SPHERES

Preparation Time: 20 minutes - **Cooking Time:** 5 minutes - **Servings:** 6-8

INGREDIENTS:

- 3 cups of rolled oats
- 2 tablespoons of cocoa powder
- 1 ½ cups of cannabis-infused butter
- 3 tablespoons of honey
- ¼ cup of peanut butter

DIRECTIONS:

1. Place a saucepan over heat and add cannabis-infused butter to melt. Add all other ingredients to the pan; stir and cook for 5 minutes. Pour the mixture in a baking pan and refrigerate for 15 minutes. Roll the mixture into small balls and refrigerate again. Serve.

Nutrition: Calories: 125, Fat:1.2g, Fiber: 5g, Carbs: 38g, Protein: 1g

PAVLOV WITH CANNA-RASPBERRY SAUCE

Preparation Time: 20 minutes - **Cooking Time:** 30 minutes - **Servings:** 6

INGREDIENTS:

For the meringues

- 3 large egg whites, at room temperature
- ½ teaspoon cream of tartar
- Pinch salt
- ⅔ cup granulated sugar
- 2 teaspoons cornstarch
- 1 teaspoon white vinegar
- 1 teaspoon vanilla extract

For the raspberry sauce

- ½ cup of orange juice
- 2 teaspoons cornstarch

- 1-pound raspberries, rinsed
- ¼ cup honey
- 1 tablespoon Canna-Coconut Oil
- Pinch salt

DIRECTIONS:

1. Preheat the oven to 275°F. Line a baking sheet with parchment paper. For the meringues, in a tall, metal bowl, using an electric mixer on high speed, whip the egg whites, cream of tartar, and salt together until soft peaks form, about a minute. As you are running the mixer, gradually add the sugar, 2 tablespoons at a time. Continue to beat on high speed until stiff peaks form. If you feel the meringue between your fingers, it should be smooth. If you still feel the sugar granules, keep beating on medium speed until the sugar has fully dissolved. Add in the cornstarch, vinegar, and vanilla and whisk to incorporate. Spoon about ½ cup of the egg white mixture for each pavlova onto the prepared baking sheet. Using a spoon, spread each into a 3-inch concave circle, with higher sides and a slight hollow in the middle. You should have enough for 6 pavlovas.

2. Bake until very light tan in color, and the meringue seems set, 25 to 30 minutes. Turn off the oven, open the door a smidge, and allow the pavlovas to cool completely. For the raspberry sauce, in a small bowl, combine the orange juice and cornstarch. Stir to until smooth. Over low heat, in a small saucepan, combine the raspberries, honey, and canna-oil and mix well, mashing the raspberries into a smooth sauce as they soften. Add the cornstarch mixture, increase the heat to medium, and stir until the mixture begins to thicken, 4 to 5 minutes; the sauce will continue to thicken as it cools. Stir in the salt. Put it away from the heat and pour into a small pitcher. Top the pavlovas with equal portions of the raspberry sauce immediately before serving.

3. Storage: You can prepare the pavlovas hours in advance and store them in an airtight container at room temperature until ready to serve. The sauce can also be made in advance and stored in the refrigerator, covered. If the consistency is too thick and hard to pour, heat it in the microwave for 10 seconds or so. Once sauced, you need to eat the pavlovas immediately.

Nutrition: Calories: 215, Fat:2.7g, Fiber: 1.7g, Carbs: 53g, Protein: 1.2g

CHOCOLATE OLIVE OIL CAKE

Preparation Time: 15 minutes - **Cooking Time:** 30 minutes - **Servings:** 6-8

INGREDIENTS:

- 3 cups all-purpose flour
- 2 cups of sugar
- 6 tablespoons good-quality cocoa powder
- 2 teaspoons baking soda

- 1 teaspoon salt
- ½ cup finely chopped nuts or dried fruit (optional)
- ¾ cup canna oil
- 2 tablespoons white vinegar
- 1 tablespoon vanilla
- 2 cups cold water Powdered sugar, for dusting

DIRECTIONS:

1. Preheat the oven to 350°F. Grease and flour two 8-inch cake pans or lines a 12-cup muffin tin with muffin liners. In a bowl, put in sugar and flour, cocoa powder, baking soda, salt, and nuts or dried fruit (if using). Whisk to incorporate. In another bowl, whisk together the oil, vinegar, vanilla, and water, then add to the flour mixture. With a hand mixer on medium-low speed, mix just until smooth. Pour into the prepared cake pans or muffin tin. Bake 30 to 40 minutes for cake or 20 to 25 minutes for muffins, or until a toothpick inserted in the center comes out clean (start checking early to avoid over baking). Cool completely. Before serving, dust with powdered sugar.

Nutrition: Calories: 210, Fat: 6.8g, Fiber: 4.1, Carbs: 34.6g, Protein: 2.1g

ORANGE ALMOND CAKE

Preparation Time: 15 minutes - **Cooking Time:** 45-50 minutes - **Servings:** 6-8

INGREDIENTS:

- 2 cups packed almond flour, plus more for dusting
- 1 teaspoon baking powder
- ½ teaspoon baking soda
- 1 teaspoon ground cinnamon
- 1 teaspoon ground ginger
- ½ teaspoon salt
- 3 eggs, lightly beaten⅔ cup honey plus1 teaspoon, divided
- ¼ cup canna oil
- Zest and juice (¼ cup) of 1 orange
- 1 cup fresh raspberries
- Whipped cream, chopped toasted almonds or pistachios, and powdered sugar, for garnish

DIRECTIONS:

1. Preheat the oven to 325°F. Grease a 9-inch spring form pan and dust the inside with almond flour. In a large bowl, whisk together the almond flour, baking powder, baking soda, cinnamon, ginger, and salt. In another bowl, whisk together the eggs, ⅔ cup of the honey, oil, and orange zest. The dry

ingredients will then be added to the egg mixture and fold in until just a few lumps remain, then gently fold in the raspberries. Put the mixture in the prepared pan and smoothen the top part. Bake for 45 to 50 minutes, or until the edges are browned, and the center is set. Warm the remaining 1 teaspoon honey with the orange juice. Brush this onto the warm cake—it'll sink right in—then let it cool completely in the pan. To serve, garnish slices with whipped cream, chopped almonds or pistachios, and a dusting of powdered sugar.

Nutrition: Calories: 219, Fat: 5.8g, Fiber: 6.4, Carbs: 32.1g, Protein: 3.2g

CRANBERRY BREAD

Preparation Time: 15 minutes - **Cooking Time:** 50-60 minutes - **Servings:** 6-8

INGREDIENTS:

- 2 cups of the gluten-free flour mix
- 1 teaspoon of salt
- 5 teaspoons of baking powder
- 2 teaspoons of gelatin
- ½ cup of cannabutter
- ½ cup of sugar
- 3 eggs, separated
- ½ tablespoon of grated orange rind
- ¾ cup of orange juice (fresh squeezed is best)
- 1 cup of fresh cranberries, cut in half

DIRECTIONS:

1. Bring the temperature of your oven to 350. Ensure to grease and flour an 8 x 8-inch loaf pan (glass is best).

2. In a medium bowl, whisk together the gluten-free flour, salt, baking powder (gluten-free), and gelatin gum, using a wire whisk. Using a mixer set on medium-high, cream the Cannabutter or margarine and sugar until fluffy. Add the egg yolks and beat on medium-high until combined. Next, add the orange rind and then a little of the flour. Mix. Add orange juice. Mix. Repeat this process until all the flour and juice are mixed. Stir in the cranberries using a wooden spoon. Beat the egg whites until stiff and then fold them gently into the batter. Pour in the batter onto the prepared pan then place it in the center of the oven. Bake for about 50 minutes, 60 if needed. The loaf should be golden in color. When cool, cut the loaf into 12 slices. One slice should do the trick. For an extra zing spread, Cannabutter or margarine on the slice before eating.

Nutrition: Calories: 229, Fat: 5.5g, Fiber: 5g, Carbs: 39g, Protein: 4g

CANNA-BANANA BREAD

Preparation Time: 10-15 minutes **- Cooking Time:** 60 minutes **- Servings:** 4-6

INGREDIENTS:

- ½ cup of soft Cannabutter
- 1 cup of white sugar
- 2 eggs
- 1 teaspoon of vanilla extract
- 1 ½ cup of mashed banana
- 2 cups of flour
- 1 teaspoon of baking soda

DIRECTIONS:

1. Preheat the oven to 350 degrees. Grease a 9 "x 5" loaf tin and dust with flour. Beat the Cannabutter and the sugar until smooth. Add vanilla extract. Beat in the eggs and then the bananas. Stir in flour and baking powder carefully. Pour the bread batter into the pan. Bake in the preheated oven for an hour.

Nutrition: Calories: 295, Fat: 8.1g, Fiber: 2.3, Carbs: 45g, Protein: 1.8g

RED VELVET CANNA CAKE

Preparation Time: 20 minutes **- Cooking Time:** 35-40 minutes **- Servings:** 20-24

INGREDIENTS:

- 16 ounces of cream cheese
- 4 ounces of butter, softened
- 3 cups of powdered sugar
- 2 ¾ cup of purpose flour
- 1 ¾ cup of white sugar
- 1 ¼ cup of buttermilk
- ¾ cup of canola oil
- ¾ cup canna oil
- 2 eggs
- 1 tablespoon of white vinegar
- 4 teaspoons of red food coloring
- 3 teaspoons of vanilla extract
- 2 teaspoons of cocoa powder

- 1 teaspoon of baking soda
- ¼ teaspoon of salt

DIRECTIONS:

1. Before you do anything preheat the oven to 325 F. Beat the eggs with canna oil, canola oil, 1 teaspoon of vanilla extract, buttermilk and vinegar in a large mixing bowl Stir the flour with white sugar, cocoa powder, baking soda and salt. Add the mixture gradually to the buttermilk while whisking all the time until no lumps are found. Add the liquid food coloring and stir in the batter until you get a dark red batter. Pour the batter into 3 lined up and greased cake pans then cook them in the oven for 34 to 36 min. Once the time is up, allow the cakes to lose heat completely. In the meantime, beat the butter in a large mixing bowl until they become soft. Add the sugar gradually while beating all the time, followed by the cream cheese until the mix becomes soft and fluffy. Add the vanilla extract then mix them well to make the icing. Level the cakes with a sharp bread knife to make them equal with the same thickness and size. Place some icing in the middle of a cake stand and place it on top of it a cake. Spread some frosting on it, then top it with the second cake and repeat the process to with the third cake. Cover the whole cake with the rest of the frosting, then decorate it the way you desire and refrigerate it for 30 min or more. Serve your cake and enjoy it.

Nutrition: Calories: 288, Fat: 8.7g, Fiber: 2.1g, Carbs: 54g, Protein: 1.8g

CHERRY- CRANBERRY GINGER CAKE

Preparation Time: 15 minutes - **Cooking Time:** 35 -40 minutes - **Servings:** 4-6

INGREDIENTS:

- 1½ cups Dark Cherries drained, chopped-set aside
- 2 cups whole wheat white cake flour
- ½ teaspoon ground ginger
- 2 tablespoons chopped crystallized ginger
- ¼ teaspoon salt
- 1½ teaspoons baking powder
- ½ cup cranberries
- ½ cup apricots, chopped
- ¾ cup canna milk
- 2 eggs
- ¼ cup stevia
- 3 tablespoons molasses
- ¼ cup coconut oil softened

DIRECTIONS:

1. Prepare a lightly greased and lined with parchment paper 9-inch cake pan. In a bowl, put all dry ingredients together and mix well. Then, in another bowl, put all wet ingredients and mix with a whisk. Combine egg mixture and flour and blend Fold in cherries and bake at 350°F for30-35 minutes.

Nutrition: Calories: 256, Fat: 6.5g, Fiber: 4g, Carbs: 41.2g, Protein: 1.7g

PEACH JELLY ROLL

Preparation Time: 15-20 minutes   **- Cooking Time:** 60 minutes **- Servings:** 6-8

INGREDIENTS:

- 2¼ cups whole wheat pastry flour
- ¼ cup wheat bran, unprocessed
- ½ teaspoon baking powder
- ¼ teaspoon baking soda
- ½ teaspoon salt
- ½ cup canna coconut oil, slightly softened but still firm
- ¾ cup yogurt
- ¼ cup milk
- 8 cups peaches, thinly sliced
- 1 cup dates, minced
- ¼ cup honey

DIRECTIONS:

1. In a bowl, combine all the prepared dry ingredients and mix well. Mix in coconut oil and slowly add other wet ingredients except for peaches, dates and honey, for the remaining three ingredients, mix all of it and set aside. Divide dough in two and roll each on a floured surface into a rectangle shape
2. Split peaches in half and top each section of rolled dough, leaving edges free. Roll up without letting peaches fall out and pinch to seal. In a greased pan, bake, covered at 350°F for 30 minutes and uncovered for an additional 30 minutes.

Nutrition: Calories: 210, Fat: 6.8g, Fiber: 4.1, Carbs: 34.6g, Protein: 2.1g

SILKY COCONUT CAKE

Preparation Time: 15-20 minutes **- Cooking Time:** 30-40 minutes **- Servings:** 6-8

INGREDIENTS:

- 2 cups whole wheat cake flour
- 2 teaspoons baking powder
- ½ cup toasted wheat bran
- ½ teaspoon baking soda
- 3 teaspoons lemon zest
- ½ cup of cocoa powder
- ½ teaspoon salt
- 2 large eggs
- ½ cup molasses
- ½ cup dark honey
- ½ cup apple juice
- ½ cup of coconut oil at room temperature
- ¾ cup dark chocolate chips
- Chocolate Frosting (optional)

DIRECTIONS:

1. In a bowl, combine all the prepared dry ingredients and mix well. Same goes with all the wet ingredients, slowly add together using whisk; egg mixture, flour mixture and 1 cup boiling water, a little at a time until totally incorporated; do not over mix Stir in chocolate chips then fold. Pour cake in a lined 12-inch round spring form pan and bake at 350°F for 30-40 minutes until springs back when you press. Cool then frost with chocolate frosting.

Nutrition: Calories: 245, Fat: 8g, Fiber: 4.3g, Carbs: 30.9g, Protein: 2.6g

CANNABIS STRAWBERRY CAKE

Preparation Time: 20 minutes - **Cooking Time:** 40 minutes - **Servings:** 12

INGREDIENTS:

- Nonstick baking spray
- 10 tablespoons (1¼ sticks) unsalted butter, melted
- 2 tablespoons Canna-Butter, melted
- 1¼ cups plus 2 tablespoons granulated sugar, divided
- 2 large eggs, lightly beaten
- 1 tablespoon orange juice concentrate
- 2 teaspoons grated orange zest
- ½ teaspoon almond extract
- 1½ cups gluten-free 1-to-1 baking flour

- ½ cup plus 1 tablespoon strawberry jam, divided
- 1 cup slivered or sliced almonds
- 1½ cups vanilla Greek yogurt

DIRECTIONS:

1. Preheat the oven to 340°F.Using a nonstick spray or butter and flour, Coat a 9-inch square baking pan. In a large bowl, combine the melted butter and 1¼ cups of sugar. Stir in the beaten eggs and mix well. Stir in the orange juice concentrate, zest, and almond extract. Stir in the flour until just mixed. Pour the batter into the prepared pan. Using a knife, swirl ½ cup of the jam into the batter toward the center. Sprinkle with the almonds, then the remaining 2 tablespoons sugar. Bake until golden and set, 35 to 40 minutes. Once completely cooled slice into 12 equal pieces. In a small bowl, combine the yogurt with the remaining 1 tablespoon jam and place a dollop on each slice.

Nutrition: Calories: 341, Fat: 8.1g, Fiber: 6g, Carbs: 41.7g, Protein: 1.7g

STONER'S LEMON POPPY SEED LOAF

Preparation Time: 20 minutes **- Cooking Time:** 55-65 min **- Servings:** 6-8

INGREDIENTS:

- 1 ¾ cups All-purpose flour
- ¾ cup Cannabis Butter* melted
- 1 tablespoon poppy seeds
- 1 cup Granulated sugar
- 1 teaspoon Baking powder
- 2/3 cup Milk
- 2 Eggs 1 teaspoon Vanilla
- 1 tablespoon Lemon zest
- ½ teaspoon Salt
- For the Glaze
- ½ cup icing sugar
- 1 tablespoon Lemon juice

DIRECTIONS:

1. Preheat oven the oven to 350 F. Grease a 9 × 5 in. Loaf pan. Mix flour with sugar, poppy seeds, lemon zest, baking powder and salt in a bowl. Cream the Cannabis Butter* with milk, eggs and vanilla in a large bowl, using a whisk or an electric mixer on medium, until smooth and creamy in texture, Then, blend in flour mixture and mix until just combined. Don't over-mix. Pour the mixture into a loaf pan. Bake and check if it is cooked by inserting a wooden skewer or toothpick in the

center of the loaf and when it comes out clean, around 55 to 65 min. Transfer pan to a cooling rack, and let stand 10 min. Meanwhile, do the glaze, Whisk icing sugar with lemon juice in a small bowl. Brush glaze over warm loaf. Let stand until loaf is cool, about 2 hours.

Nutrition: Calories: 290, Fat: 3.5, Fiber: 4.1, Carbs: 45g, Protein: 4.6g

CHOCO-ESPRESSO SPELT CAKE

Preparation Time: 30 minutes - **Cooking Time:** 1 hr. - **Servings:** 8-12

INGREDIENTS:

- 2 cups spelt flour
- 3/4 cup cannabutter
- 3/4 cup cocoa powder
- 1 cup packed dark brown sugar
- 2 large eggs
- 1 cup boiling-hot water
- 1 1/2 tablespoons instant espresso powder
- 1 teaspoon baking soda
- 1 1/2 cups dates (12 to 14), pitted and coarsely chopped
- 2 teaspoons baking powder
- 3/4 teaspoon salt
- 1 1/2 teaspoons vanilla extract

DIRECTIONS:

1. Preheat oven to 350F. Grease spring form pan, then lightly dust with cocoa powder, removing out excess. Mix together boiling-hot water, espresso powder, vanilla, and baking soda in a bowl, then add dates, mashing lightly with a fork, and slightly simmer then cool down to room temperature, about 10 minutes. Blend together spelt flour, cocoa powder, baking powder, and salt in another bowl. Cream together canna butter and brown sugar until pale and fluffy. Put in the eggs one at a time. Add in date mixture and add the flour a little at a time, mixing until just combined. Spoon batter into a spring form pan, smoothing top, and bake until a wooden pick or skewer inserted into the center comes out clean, about 50 minutes to 1 hour. Cool down the cake by transferring it to a rack for a few minutes, then remove side of the pan and cool cake on rack. Serve cake warm or at room temperature.

Nutrition: Calories: 280, Fat: 6.1g, Fiber: 4.3g, Carbs: 39.1g, Protein: 5g

CANNA CINNAMON COFFEE CAKE

Preparation Time: 20 minutes - **Cooking Time:** 30 minutes - **Servings:** 4-6

INGREDIENTS:

- 1 1/4 cups flour (cannabis flour extra potency)
- 1/4 cup cannabutter
- 1/2 cup sugar
- 1/4 cup sour cream
- 1/3 cup canna milk or regular milk
- 2 eggs, slightly beaten
- 2 tsp. baking powder
- tsp. cinnamon
- Topping:
- 1/3 cup flour
- 1/3 cup brown sugar
- 1/4 cup cannabutter
- 1 tsp. cinnamon powder

DIRECTIONS:

1. First, preheat the oven to 375 degrees Fahrenheit, subsequently combining all ingredients for the cake batter in a large mixing bowl. After thoroughly mixing, pour the batter into an 8 or 9-inch greased or buttered pan. After this, combine the flour and brown sugars for the topping in a big bowl, mixing in the cannabutter and cinnamon after. Mix until it becomes chunky and crumbly. Spread over the batter and bake for 28-30 minutes.

Nutrition: Calories: 311, Fat: 7,5g, Fiber: 3g, Carbs: 40.1g, Protein: 5g

CANNA APPLE PECAN SPACE CAKE

Preparation Time: 20 minutes - **Cooking Time:** 45 minutes - **Servings:** 4-6

INGREDIENTS:

- 1 cup flour
- 1/2 cup whole wheat flour
- 1/4 tsp. cinnamon
- 1/2 tsp. baking soda
- 1/2 tsp. nutmeg
- 1/2 tsp. salt

- 1 egg
- 1 cup granulated
- 2/3 cup canna oil
- 1/2 cup pecans chopped
- 2 apples, peeled and grated
- 1 gala apple, thinly sliced
- 15 pecan halves
- For the glaze:
- 1/4 cup brown sugar
- 2 tsp. cannabis oil
- 2 tsp. water

DIRECTIONS:

1. Heat your oven to 325 degrees Fahrenheit. Lightly coat a 9-inch spring form pan with nonstick cooking spray, In a medium bowl, combine the cinnamon, flours, baking soda, nutmeg and salt until blended. Whisk sugar and egg with the 2/3 cup cannabis-infused olive oil in a bowl. Stir the flour mixture into the egg mixture, and add the chopped pecans and grated apples. Scrape into the prepared pan and flatten the top of it, Arrange the apple slices on top of the edge of the cake, and arrange the pecan halves in one layer in the center.
2. Make the glaze in a small bowl. Mix together the brown sugar and the 2 tsp. olive oil and water and microwave in thirty-second intervals until the brown sugar is melted. Brush the apples and pecan with half of the glaze and save the rest.
3. Bake in the center of the oven until a toothpick when inserted in the middle of the cake comes out clean. Remove the pan out of the oven and brush the top of the warm cake with the rest of the glaze. Gently remove the cake from the base then serve.

Nutrition: Calories: 290, Fat: 7.2g, Fiber: 4.1, Carbs: 46g, Protein: 3.4g

CANNA CARROT MUFFINS

Preparation Time: 15 minutes - **Cooking Time:** 25-30 minutes - **Servings:** 10-12

INGREDIENTS:

- 1¾ cups flour
- 1 teaspoon salt
- 1 teaspoon cinnamon
- 1teaspoon ground ginger
- ½ teaspoon grated nutmeg

- ¼ teaspoon baking soda
- ⅛ teaspoon baking powder
- 1 cup maple syrup
- ½ cup solid CBD Coconut Oil melted, or ¼ cup CBD Oil mixed with ¼ cup vegetable oil
- ½ cup milk
- 1 tablespoon fresh lemon juice
- 1 teaspoon vanilla extract
- 2 cups grated carrot
- ½ cup crushed pineapple, drained
- ½ cup each raisin, coconut, and pecans (or any nuts you like)

DIRECTIONS:

1. Preheat the oven to 350°F. Line two 12-cup muffin tins with muffin papers or grease and flour the tins. In a large bowl, combine the flour, salt, cinnamon, ginger, nutmeg, baking soda, and baking powder. In a separate bowl, combine the maple syrup, coconut oil, milk, lemon juice, and vanilla. Combine both the wet and dry ingredients then fold it gently until just combined (over mixing makes the muffins tough). Fold in the carrots, pineapple, raisins, coconut, and pecans. Fill the prepared muffin tins two-thirds full. Let the cake bake for around 25 minutes or more or until a toothpick inserted into the center of a muffin comes out clean. Let them cool a little before serving.

Nutrition: Calories: 200, Fat: 5.1g, Fiber: 2tgg, Carbs: 25.8g, Protein: 1.2g

RUM RAISIN CUPCAKES

INGREDIENTS:

- Rum Raisins
- ¼ cup dark rum
- ½ cup golden raisins
- Cupcakes
- 1 cup all-purpose flour
- 1¼ teaspoons baking powder
- ¼ teaspoon ground cinnamon
- ⅛ teaspoon ground allspice
- ⅛ teaspoon freshly grated nutmeg
- ½ cup cannabutter, slightly softened
- 2 tablespoons unsalted butter, slightly softened
- ¾ cup firmly packed light brown sugar

- 3 large eggs
- 1 tablespoon pure vanilla extract
- ¼ teaspoon pure rum extract
- Sweet Cream Frosting
- ¼ cup unsalted butter, slightly softened
- ½ cup heavy cream
- 2 cups powdered sugar, sifted
- ⅛ teaspoon salt

DIRECTIONS:

1. Prepare the rum raisins: In a small saucepan, warm the rum over low heat. Blend in the raisins and put it away from heat. Put the mix in a bowl, and then cover it with a saran wrap and let sit at room temperature for at least 6 hours or overnight. Prepare the cupcakes: Bring the temperature of your oven to 180c Put paper liners in the muffin tin. Ina medium bowl, stir together the flour, baking powder, cinnamon, allspice, and nutmeg. Set aside. Ina large bowl using an electric mixer, beat together the cannabutter, regular butter, and brown sugar on medium to high speed until you see that it becomes light and cloudlike, gradually add eggs, beating well after each addition. Beat in the vanilla and rum extracts. Reduce the speed mixer to low, add the flour mixture, and mix until just combined. Fold in the rum raisins and any remaining liquid. Scoop up the cupcake batter into the pan. Bake it for about 20 to 25 minutes, or until golden brown and a toothpick inserted into the center of a cupcake comes out clean. Let cool in the tin for 5 minutes, and then transfer to a wire rack to cool completely. Cupcakes without frosting can be stored up to 3 months. Prepare the sweet cream frosting: In a medium bowl using an electric mixer, beat the butter on medium speed until creamy. Lower down the speed to medium and add the cream and 1 cup of the powdered sugar; beat until well combined. Slowly add the remaining1 cup sugar and the salt. Put the frosting to a piping bag fitted with the tip of your choice and frost the cupcakes, or simply frost them with a butter knife or small offset spatula. Store the frosted cupcakes in an airtight container in the refrigerator for up to 1 week.

Nutrition: Calories: 215, Fat: 5g, Fiber: 4.1, Carbs: 35.6g, Protein: 2g

HOT GANJA CHOCOLATE CUPCAKES

Preparation Time: 10 minutes - **Cooking Time:** 20-25 minutes - **Servings:** 2-4

INGREDIENTS:

- ½ Cup all-purpose flour
- 1 tsp. Baking Powder
- Pinch Salt

- 1/3 Cup Cocoa
- ½-1 t Hot Red Pepper Flakes
- 2 tbsp. canna oil
- Scant ½ Cup of milk
- ½ tsp. Vanilla
- ¼ tsp. Apple Cider Vinegar
- ¼ Cup Sugar

DIRECTIONS:

1. Preheat oven to 365°. Combine Flour, Baking Powder, Salt and Sugar. Whisk! Add wet ingredients and whisk until completely smooth. Fill 4-5 cupcake liners 2/3 full. Bake for 20 minutes or until a toothpick comes out clean. Allow to cool completely before frosting.

Nutrition: Calories: 187, Fat: 4.3g, Fiber: 2g, Carbs: 29.6g, Protein: 1g

FRENCH TOAST CUPCAKES

Preparation Time: 20 minutes - **Cooking Time:** 20-25 minutes - **Servings:** 12

INGREDIENTS:

- Topping
- ¼ cup all-purpose flour
- ¼ cup of sugar
- 2½ tablespoons unsalted butter, cut into ½-inch pieces and chilled
- ½ teaspoon ground cinnamon
- ¼ cup chopped pecans
- Cupcakes
- 1½ cups all-purpose flour
- 1 cup of sugar
- 1½ teaspoons baking powder
- 1 teaspoon ground cinnamon
- ½ teaspoon ground allspice
- ¼ teaspoon freshly grated nutmeg
- ½ teaspoon salt
- ½ cup cannabutter slightly softened
- ½ cup sour cream
- 2 large eggs
- ½ teaspoon maple extract

- 4 slices bacon

DIRECTIONS:

1. First the topping must be prepared. In a medium bowl, blend in sugar, flour, cinnamon, walnuts and butter. Using your fingers, blend in the butter until there are no pieces bigger than a little pea. Cover and refrigerate until prepared to use. Set up the cupcakes: Preheat your stove to 350°F. Line a 12-cup biscuit tin with paper liners. In an enormous bowl, whisk together the flour, sugar, preparing powder, cinnamon, allspice, nutmeg, and salt. Put in a safe spot. In a huge bowl utilizing an electric blender, beat together the cannabutter, cream, eggs, and maple syrup on medium speed until the blend is mixed well. Lessen the blender speed to low and include the flour blend. Beat until simply consolidated. Fill each well of the biscuit tin 2/3 full, bake it for around 20 to 25 minutes or until a toothpick embedded into the focal point of a cupcake tells the truth. While the cupcakes are heating, cook the bacon as how you like it done. Move to a paper towel to drip the excess oil and let cool. Cupcakes must be chilled off in the tin for around 15 minutes. At that point, move to a wire rack to cool totally. Cut the bacon into 12 pieces and press a piece into the top of each muffin. For storing muffins in the freezer, seal it tightly, and it can last up to 3 months, just omit the bacon. Reheat in the toaster oven for extra deliciousness.

Nutrition: Calories: 190, Fat: 5g, Fiber: 3g, Carbs: 28.8g, Protein: 1.7g

CANNABIS HUMMINGBIRD CUPCAKES

Preparation Time: 10-15 minutes - **Cooking Time:** 15-20 minutes - **Servings:** 12

INGREDIENTS:

- 2 large ripe bananas, mashed
- 1 cup of all-purpose
- 1/2 tsp. baking powder
- 1/3 cup pineapple (crushed (do not drain)
- 1/2 tsp. baking soda
- 1/2 tsp. ground cinnamon
- 1/4 tsp. salt
- ½ cup cannabutter, at room temperature
- 1/2 cup sugar
- 2 large eggs
- 1 tsp. pure vanilla extract
- 1/2 cup chopped pecans
- 1 cup unsweetened desiccated coconut

- 1/2 cup golden raisins (optional)
- Cream Cheese Frosting
- 8 ounces cream cheese, at room temperature
- 1/4 cup butter, at room temperature
- 3 cups powdered sugar
- 2 teaspoons vanilla extract

DIRECTIONS:

1. Preheat your oven to 350 degrees placing the rack in the center. Line a 12-cup muffin pan with cupcake liners in preparation. Combine the bananas and pineapples in a bowl. Mash together with the back of a fork and set aside. Whisk or beat together the flour, baking powder, baking soda, cinnamon and salt in a separate medium bowl. Add the cannabutter and the sugar to a large bowl. Beat with a whisk until the mixture is fluffy and light. Gradually put the eggs and then the vanilla extract. Add the dry ingredients into the wet by scoopfuls and beat until thoroughly combined.

2. Stir in the pineapple and bananas, being careful not to over-mix. Fold in the pecans, coconut and golden raisins (if using). Pour batter into the liners, working to fill at least 2/3 of the way. Put it inside the oven and let it bake for around 30 to 40 minutes. The signs of completed cupcakes will include a toothpick that comes out clean and an outwardly golden appearance.

3. Remove from the oven and place on a wire rack to cool. Once this is achieved, use a small spatula or kitchen knife to frost tops of each cupcake. Top with finely chopped pecans.

4. Frosting (Cream-cheese)

5. Put the cream cheese and the butter in a bowl then and beat together with a whisk until very smooth and no lumps. Then add in the vanilla extract and fine sugar, continuously beating until it is light and smooth.

Nutrition: Calories: 216, Fat: 3.1g, Fiber: 1.4g, Carbs: 56g, Protein: 4

KIRSCH CHOCOLATE MUFFINS

Preparation Time: 15 minutes - **Cooking Time:** 20-25 minutes - **Servings:** 6-8

INGREDIENTS:

- 1/2 tsp. baking soda
- 1/2 cup of cannabutter
- ½ cup of roughly cut dark chocolate
- 3/4 cup of brown sugar
- 1/4 cup of either unsweetened cocoa powder (Dutch cocoa works too)
- 3/4 cup of milk

- 1 1/4 cups of self-rising flour
- 2 eggs
- 15 ounces of dark cherries in syrup (thawed, drained, whatever the preference)
- 1 tbsp. cocoa
- Extra 1 tsp. icing sugar

DIRECTIONS:

1. Set the oven to 350°F. Prepare a 12-hole muffin tray with liners. Cream the butter and sugar together, adding a single egg at a time. Take the baking soda, the cocoa, and the flour and sift together with the butter mix from before. Finish up by combining with the milk, chocolate, and cherries. Try to fill each cupcake tin to approximately ¾ full and place in the preheated oven for 20-25 minutes. A sign that cupcakes are done is by doing the clean toothpick test. Once it is cooked, put it away from heat and let cool while the icing is made. Frost and enjoy it!

Nutrition: Calories: 196, Fat: 4.2g, Fiber: 1.8, Carbs: 30.6g, Protein: 1.1g

CANNA- BANANA CRUMBLE MUFFINS

Preparation Time: 10-15 minutes - **Cooking Time:** 18-20 minutes - **Servings:** 8-10

INGREDIENTS:

- 1 ½ cups flour
- 1/3 cup cannabis butter
- 3 mashed bananas
- 3/4 cup cane sugar
- 1/3 cup packed brown sugar
- 1 tsp. baking soda
- 1 tsp. baking powder
- 1/2 tsp. table salt
- 1 egg
- 2 tbsp. flour
- 1 tbsp. butter
- 1/8 tsp. ground cinnamon

DIRECTIONS:

1. Bring the heat of your oven to 350 f. and lightly butter a 10-cup muffin tray. Get out a large mixing bowl and mix the 1.5 cups flour, baking soda, baking powder and salt. In a separate bowl, mix the mashed bananas, egg, cane sugar and 1/3 cup melted cannabis butter. Stir this mixture into the first mixture until just blended. Spread this batter evenly into the greased or buttered muffin cups. In

another bowl, combine the brown sugar, cinnamon and 2 tbsp. Flour. Cut in 1 tbsp. Butter. Sprinkle this mixture over the muffin batter in the trays. Bake 18 - 20 minutes; allow cooling on a wire rack and enjoying.

Nutrition: Calories: 210, Fat: 6g, Fiber: 2.4, Carbs: 35g, Protein: 1.7 g

LEMON COCONUT MUFFINS

Preparation Time: 10-15 minutes - **Cooking Time:** 15-20 minutes - **Servings:** 8-10

INGREDIENTS:

- 1 1/4 cup almond flour
- 1 cup shredded unsweetened coconut
- 2 tbsp. coconut flour
- 1/2 tsp. baking soda
- 1/2 tsp. baking powder
- 1/4 tsp. salt
- 1/4 cup of honey (raw)
- Juice and zest from 1 lemon
- 1/4 cup full-fat coconut milk
- 3 eggs, whisked
- 3 tbsp. medicated coconut oil
- 1 tsp. vanilla extract

DIRECTIONS:

1. Bring the heat of your oven to 350 f. In a small bowl, mix all the wet ingredients together. In a medium bowl, combine all the dry ingredients. Now pour the wet ingredients into the dry ingredients bowl and stir into a batter. Let your batter sit for a few minutes then stir it again. Now grease a muffin tin and fill each about two-thirds of the way full. Pop it in the oven and bake for about 20 minutes. Test the doneness of the muffin by inserting a toothpick in the center, and if it comes out clean, that means you are good to go. Remove from oven, let cool for a cool minute and serve!

Nutrition: Calories: 296, Fat: 7,5g, Fiber: 3.2, Carbs: 50g, Protein: 1.9g

MARIJUANA OATMEAL BARS

Preparation Time: 15 minutes - **Cooking Time:** 25-30 minutes - **Servings:** 14-16

INGREDIENTS:

- 1¼ cups old-fashioned rolled oats

- 1¼ cups all-purpose flour
- ½ cup finely chopped toasted walnuts (see Note)
- ½ cup of sugar
- ½ teaspoon baking soda
- ¼ teaspoon sal t
- 1 cup cannabutter, melted
- 2 teaspoons vanilla
- 1 cup good-quality jam
- 4 whole graham crackers (8 squares), crushed
- Whipped cream, for serving (optional)

DIRECTIONS:

1. Preheat the oven to 350°F. Grease a 9-inch square baking pan. In a bowl, put in and combine oatmeal, flour, walnuts, sugar, baking soda, and salt. In a small bowl, combine the butter and vanilla. Add the butter mixture to the oat mixture and mix until crumbly. Reserve 1 cup for topping, and press the remaining oat mixture into the bottom of the baking pan. Spread the jam evenly over the top. Add the crushed crackers to the reserved oat mixture and sprinkle over the jam. Bake it for around 25 to 30 minutes, or until the edges are browned. Cool completely in the pan on a rack. Cut into 16 squares. Serve, adding a dollop of whipped cream if desired. Storing it in a glass container in the fridge will help preserve it.

Nutrition: Calories: 299, Fat: 6.8g, Fiber: 4.1, Carbs: 67g, Protein: 3.1

JANE'S CHEWY PECAN BARS

Preparation Time: 20 minutes - **Cooking Time:** 1 hr. and 15 minutes

INGREDIENTS:

- Nonstick baking spray
- 2 cups plus
- 2 tablespoons all-purpose flour, divided
- ½ cup granulated sugar
- 2 tablespoons plus
- 2 tsp. cannabutter
- 3½ teaspoons unsalted butter, cut into pieces
- ¾ teaspoon plus kosher pinch salt, divided
- ¾ cup packed dark brown sugar
- 4 large eggs

- 2 teaspoons vanilla extract
- 1 cup light corn syrup
- 2 cups chopped pecans
- Pecan nuts cut in half

DIRECTIONS:

1. Preheat the oven to 340°F. Grease the pan using a nonstick spray and line with parchment paper with an overhang on two sides so you can easily lift the bars from the pan. (The filling is sticky and can make it hard to remove without the parchment.)
2. By utilizing a blender or food processor, pulse flour, the sugar, kinds of butter, and ¾ teaspoon of salt until combined. The mixture will form into clumps. Transfer the dough to the prepared pan. Press it firmly and evenly in the bottom of the pan. Pierce the crust all over with a fork and bake until light to a medium golden brown, 30 to 35 minutes.
3. Using the same food processor bowl, combine the brown sugar, the remaining 2 tablespoons flour, pinch salt, eggs, vanilla, and corn syrup. (Add the corn syrup last, so it doesn't get stuck on the bottom of the food processor.) Pulse until completely combined. Turn the mixture into a large bowl and add the pecans. Spoon the pecan mixture evenly over the baked crust. Place a few extra pecan halves on the top of the filling as decoration.
4. Place the pan back into the oven and let it bake until the center is just set 35 to 40 minutes. On the off chance that the inside still wiggles, prepare for a couple of more minutes; if you notice the bars are beginning to puff in the center, remove them right away. Put them in a rack and leave to cool before cutting into 16 (2-inch) squares and lifting the bars out.
5. Storage: Keep the bars in an airtight container at room temperature for 3 to 5 days or freeze for up to 6 months. They can be very sticky, so wrap them in parchment or wax paper.

Nutrition: Calories: 190, Fat: 1.5g, Fiber: 4.1, Carbs: 26g, Protein: 1g

ORANGE CREAMSICLE COOKIES

Preparation Time: 10 minutes **- Cooking Time:** 10-15 minutes **- Servings:** 24 pcs

INGREDIENTS:

- 14 tablespoons (1¾ sticks) unsalted butter, softened
- 2 tablespoons cannabutter, softened
- ½ cup granulated sugar
- ½ cup packed light brown sugar
- 1 large egg, at room temperature
- 1½ tablespoons orange juice

- 2¼ cups all-purpose flour
- 2 tablespoons grated orange zest
- 1 teaspoon baking soda
- ½ teaspoon salt
- 2 cups white chocolate chips

DIRECTIONS:

1. Preheat the oven to 340°F. Put parchment paper on the baking sheet. By utilizing an electric mixer or stand mixer on medium speed, beat the kinds of butter and both sugars together for about 2 minutes. Add the egg and orange juice and mix for 30 seconds. Add the flour, zest, baking soda, and salt, and mix on low speed, increasing to medium-low speed, until the dough comes together. Stir in the chocolate chips until incorporated. Drop heaping 2-tablespoon scoops of the dough 2 inches apart onto the prepared baking sheets. Bake the cookies until lightly golden, which may take about 8 to 10 minutes. Let cool for 3 minutes on the baking sheet, and then transfer the cookies to a wire rack to finish cooling.

2. Storage: Keep the cookies in an airtight container for 4 to 5 days or freeze for up to 6 months.

Nutrition: Calories: 275, Fat: 2g, Fiber: 4.1, Carbs: 26.4g, Protein: 1.6g

CARAMEL CRUNCH BARS

INGREDIENTS:

- 1½ cups rolled oats
- 1½ cups flour
- ¾ cup brown sugar
- ½ teaspoon baking soda
- ¼ teaspoon salt
- ¼ cup melted cannabutter
- ¼ cup melted butter
- Toppings
- ½ cup brown sugar
- ½ cup granulated sugar
- ½ cup butter
- ¼ cup flour
- 1 cup chopped nuts
- 1 cup chopped chocolate

DIRECTIONS:

1. Bring the temperature of your oven to 350 F. Put oats, flour, salt, sugar and baking soda in a bowl then mix well. Put in your cannabutter and the regular butter and mix until it forms crumbs. Put aside at least a cup of these crumbs for garnish later. Now prepare the pan by greasing it with a spray then put the oat mixture on the bottom part of the pan. Put it in the oven and bake for a while, then remove it once it is quite brown then let it cool. Then next is to make the caramel. Do this by stirring the butter and sugar in a saucepan that has a thick bottom to avoid it from burning quickly. Allow it bubble then after adding in the flour. Back to the oatmeal base, add the mixed nuts and chocolate followed by the caramel you just made, and then lastly, top it off with the extra crumbs you set aside. Place it back in the oven and let it cook until the bars are golden in color, which will take for about 20 minutes. After baking, cool it down before you cut into whatever size you want.

Nutrition: Calories: 196, Fat: 2.8g, Fiber: 3g, Carbs: 31g, Protein: 1.8 g

MARIJUANA SNOWBALLS

Preparation Time: 1 ½ hr. **- Cooking Time:** 20-25 minutes **- Servings:** 12

INGREDIENTS:

- 1 cup cannabutter, softened
- 1/4 cup sugar
- 1 tsp. pure vanilla extract
- 2 cups all-purpose flour
- 2 Tbsp. cornstarch
- 1 cup of unsalted roasted almonds, finely chopped
- 1/4 tsp. salt
- 1 cup of powdered sugar to coat

DIRECTIONS:

1. By utilizing a stand mixer or a hand mixer, beat the cannabutter with 1/4 cup of the sugar until creamy. Add the vanilla extract. Gently beat in the flour, corn starch, roasted almonds and salt until well combined. Wrap in plastic wrap and refrigerate for one hour. Preheat oven to 325°. Take the chilled dough out from the fridge and get about a tbsp. of dough then shape it into a 1-inch ball. Arrange the balls on the baking sheet about 1 inch apart. Bake the cookies on the middle shelf of the oven for 20 minutes, or until golden and set. Fill a shallow bowl with 1 cup of sifted powdered sugar. Cool for around 5 minutes, and when cool enough to touch, roll the cookies in the powdered sugar and set aside on the parchment-lined rack to cool completely. When cool, dust again in the powdered sugar and store in an airtight container.

2. Note: You can also use pecans, walnuts, hazelnuts, macadamia, almonds or any of your favorite nuts

in place of the almonds or a combination as they all work well.

Nutrition: Calories: 215, Fat: 5.8g, Fiber: 2g, Carbs: 41g, Protein: 0.7g

CITRUS POPPY SEED COOKIES

Preparation Time: 15 minutes - **Cooking Time:** 10-15 minutes - **Servings:** 36 pcs

INGREDIENTS:

- 1/2 tsp. of baking soda
- 1 tbsp. of orange zest
- 1 tsp. orange juice
- 1 tbsp. of poppy seeds
- 1/2 cup of cannabutter
- 2/3 cup of sugar
- 1 1/4 cup of flour
- 1 egg
- Dash of salt

DIRECTIONS:

1. Set the oven to 350°F for preheating. Whisk the sugar and cannabutter together for about 2 minutes. This will leave a light batter, relatively fluffy. Add the orange zest, the orange juice, and the egg, making sure to mix each one for best results thoroughly. Take another bowl and sift the baking soda, salt, and flour together. Add the sifted mixture to the original batter, and mix only long enough to see them combined before folding in the poppy seeds.
2. Tip: For chewier cookies, line the cookie sheets before baking. Parchment paper works best!
3. The mix is now ready to be placed onto the cookie sheets. Take a teaspoon and parcel out the pieces, making sure to leave even spaces between each cookie. Place in the oven and bake for about 10-12 minutes, the cookies are ultimately done when the edges are golden. Remove from the heat, let them cool down, and enjoy!

Nutrition: Calories: 216, Fat: 6.1g, Fiber: 4.1, Carbs: 35g, Protein: 1g

GANJA GINGER COOKIES

Preparation Time: 35-40 minutes - **Cooking Time:** 8-10 minutes - **Servings:** 10-12

INGREDIENTS:

- 2 cups self-rising flour
- 2 tbsp. ground ginger powder

- ¾ tbsp. ground cinnamon
- ½ tbsp. ground cloves
- ¼ tsp. salt
- ¾ cup cannabutter
- 1 cup white sugar
- 1 egg
- 1 tbsp. water
- 4 tbsp. molasses

DIRECTIONS:

1. Preheat your oven to the temperature of 180c. Sift the ginger, flour, baking soda, cloves, cinnamon and salt together. Cream the butter with the sugar in a separate bowl and beat the egg in. Add the molasses and water, and stir to mix. Add the dry ingredients gradually, stirring to combine. Spoon the mix onto plastic wrap and roll into a sausage shape. Leave for about 30 minutes to harden off. Slice the roll into rounds about 1 inch thick and place them onto an ungreased sheet, about 2 inches apart. Flatten each round a little. Back for about 8 to 10 minutes and then leave to cool for 5 minutes before transferring to a wire rack

Nutrition: Calories: 188, Fat: 3.2g, Fiber: 2g, Carbs: 29,9g, Protein: 0.5g

CANNABIS OATMEAL COOKIES

Preparation Time: 10 minutes - **Cooking Time:** 20 minutes - **Servings:** 2

INGREDIENTS:

- 1/4 cup of cannabis butter
- 2 cups packed dark brown sugar
- 1 cup (2 sticks) salted butter, softened
- 2 teaspoons of vanilla extract
- 1 1/2 cups all-purpose flour
- 1 teaspoon of salt
- 1/2 teaspoon of baking soda
- 3 cups of old-fashioned oats

DIRECTIONS:

1. Preheat your oven to the temperature of 180c. Using a bowl, beat the brown sugar and both butter until fluffy. Beat in the vanilla. Gradually add the egg into the mixture then scrape the bowl after each bowl. Mix the flour, salt and baking soda in a medium bowl. Add it to the creamy mixture in 2 to 3 servings, mix until just combined. Mix the oats until just combined. Use your preferred cookie

spoon (or a regular spoon) to drop portions of dough onto baking sheets, with spacing in between. Bake it for 12 to 13 minutes or until cookies are chewy and set.

Nutrition: Calories: 214, Fat: 3g, Fiber: 2.1, Carbs: 43g, Protein: 0.9g

JAM THUMBPRINT COOKIES

Preparation Time: 15 minutes **- Cooking Time:** 15-20 minutes **- Servings:** 3-4

INGREDIENTS:

- 1 ¼ Cups all-purpose flour
- Dash Salt
- 1/3 Cup Pure Cane Sugar
- 4 tbsp. cannabutter melted
- ½ tsp. vanilla
- ¼ Cup milk (room temp)
- Peanut Butter and/or Jelly
- Any type of jam or nut butter

DIRECTIONS:

1. Preheat your oven to the temperature of 180c. Put parchment paper in a pan or cookie sheet and put aside. Combine flour, salt & sugar. Whisk! Add melted cannabutter, vanilla and milk. Mix and knead the dough until smooth. Pull 1" chunks off of the dough ball, and roll them into spheres. Place cookies on parchment paper and press center with your thumb. Fill thumb divot with Peanut Butter and Jelly. Bake until golden (about 15-20 minutes).

Nutrition: Calories: 150, Fat: 2.1g, Fiber: 1g, Carbs: 28.5g, Protein: 0.7g

SUMMER STRAWBERRY COOKIES

Preparation Time: 15 minutes **- Cooking Time:** 10-12 minutes **- Servings:** 12

INGREDIENTS:

- ½ cup of canna Butter
- 1½ cups of flour
- ½ teaspoon of baking powder
- 1 package of strawberry gelatin
- 1 teaspoon of vanilla extract
- 1 egg

DIRECTIONS:

1. Preheat oven to 350° F. Cream the Baked Butter or margarine and gelatin in a bowl.

2. In another bowl, mix the baking powder, flour, egg, and vanilla extract together. Add this mixture to the cream of butter and gelatin; beat with an electric mixer for about 2 minutes.

3. Roll out the dough and cut it into square shapes. Place the cut cookies on a non-greased cookie sheet. Bake cookies in the oven for about 10 to 12 minutes. Let them cool. One to two cookies should do the trick.

Nutrition: Calories: 215, Fat: 4g, Fiber: 1.4g, Carbs: 31g, Protein: 1.1g

ITALIAN MANDORLA COOKIES

Preparation Time: 15 minutes - **Cooking Time:** 12-15 minutes - **Servings:** 14-18

INGREDIENTS:

- 1/2 cup of cannabutter
- 1 cup of sugar
- 1 egg
- 1 teaspoon of almond extract
- 2 cups of all-purpose flour, sifted
- 1 teaspoon of baking powder
- 2 tablespoons of Marijuana Milk
- 1 cup of chopped almonds
- 1/3 cup of apricot jams

DIRECTIONS:

1. Cream the canna Butter, sugar, egg and almond extract together in a large mixing bowl. Add the flour, baking powder and milk then blend together well. Roll small amounts of dough for each cookie. Roll each ball between your palms like you would for peanut butter cookies or even meatballs. Roll the balls in the chopped almonds and place them on greased cookie sheets. Make an indentation with your thumb or the back of a spoon and fill the dent with jam. Bake for 12 to 15 minutes. Two cookies should get you baked.

Nutrition: Calories: 177, Fat: 3.1g, Fiber: .8g, Carbs: 30.5g, Protein: 1.2g

VERY BERRY CHEESECAKE POPS

Preparation Time: 10-15 minutes - **Cooking Time:** 0 minutes - **Servings:** 4

INGREDIENTS:

- 4 ounces low-fat cream cheese

- 3/4 cup plain yogurt
- 1/4 cup agave syrup
- 1 teaspoon lemon or lime juice
- 2 gram decarboxylated kief or finely ground decarboxylated hash
- 3/4 cup fresh raspberries
- 3/4 cup fresh blueberries

DIRECTIONS:

1. Make the cream cheese light and fluffy using a stand mixer or a hand mixer. Using the low speed, add in agave syrup, yogurt, lime or lemon juice until it combined well. Next, fold in the berries using a rubber spatula. Put the mixture into popsicle molds then put them in the freezer.

Nutrition: Calories: 200, Fat: 5.9g, Fiber: 2.1, Carbs: 54.6g, Protein: 1.1g

MANGO YOGURT POPS

Preparation Time: 10 minutes - **Cooking Time:** 0 minutes - **Servings:** 4

INGREDIENTS:

- 3 tbsp. coconut sugar
- 2 mangoes, peeled and cut
- 3 tbsp. canna coconut oil
- 2 cups vanilla yogurt
- 2 tsp. coconut extract

DIRECTIONS:

1. Toss in all the ingredients in the blender. Puree until it forms a smooth mix. Transfer mix into Popsicle molds. Freeze molds.

Nutrition: Calories: 210, Fat: 7g, Fiber: 2g, Carbs: 43g, Protein: 2.1g

NUTTY BANANA YOGURT POP S

Preparation Time: 10 minutes - **Cooking Time:** 0 minutes - **Servings:** 6

INGREDIENTS:

- 1½ cups vanilla yogurt
- ¼ cup unsweetened cocoa powder
- 1 tablespoon Canna-Coconut Oil
- 1 ripe medium banana, sliced and frozen
- 1 tablespoon honey

- ½ cup chopped peanuts

DIRECTIONS:

1. In a blender, purée the yogurt, cocoa, canna-coconut oil, banana, and honey until smooth. Put the blend into another bowl and mix in the peanuts. Pour the mixture into popsicle molds and freeze until firm. Remove the pops from the molds according to the manufacturer's instructions.

2. Storage: Keep the pops in an airtight container in the freezer for up to several months.

Nutrition: Calories: 180, Fat: 1.5g, Fiber: 2.4g, Carbs: 28,9g, Protein: 0,6g

DOUBLE CHOCOLATE GELATO

Preparation Time: 15 -20 minutes **- Cooking Time:** 5 to 10 minutes **- Servings:** 4-6

INGREDIENTS:

- 1/2 cup heavy cream
- 2 cups of milk
- 3/4 cup sugar
- 1/4 teaspoon salt
- 7 ounces high-quality dark chocolate
- 1 teaspoon vanilla extract
- Cannabis butter

DIRECTIONS:

1. The first step is done by melting the chocolate, then cooling it for a bit. Place the milk, cream, and cannabis butter in a bowl and mix them together until well combined. Mix in the sugar by using a whisk and salt. Continue to whisk for about 4 minutes until the sugar and salt dissolve. Then mix in the vanilla extract. Finally, mix in the chocolate until well combined. Pour the ingredients into your ice cream maker, and let it churn for 25 minutes. Put the gelato in an airtight container and place in the freezer for up to 2 hours, until desired consistency is reached.

Nutrition: Calories: 230, Fat: 9g, Fiber: g, Carbs: 60.1g, Protein: 4g

CANNA CHERRY-STRAWBERRY GELATO

Preparation Time: 20 minutes **- Cooking Time:** 0 minutes **- Servings:** 4-6

INGREDIENTS:

- 1/2 cup heavy cream
- 2 cups of milk

- 3/4 cup sugar
- Cannabis butter*
- 1 cup sliced strawberries
- 1 tablespoon vanilla extract

DIRECTIONS:

1. Using a blender, puree the strawberry thoroughly. Place the milk, cream, and cannabis butter in a bowl and mix them together until well combined. Mix in the sugar by using a whisk. Continue to whisk for about 4 minutes until the sugar dissolves. Then mix in the vanilla extract and strawberry puree. Pour the ingredients into your ice cream maker, and let it churn for 25 minutes. Put the gelato in an airtight container and place in the freezer for up to 2 hours, until desired consistency is reached.

Nutrition: Calories: 210, Fat: 6.8g, Fiber: 6g, Carbs: 34.6g, Protein: 3g

PEACHES-N-CREAM SOFT SERVE ICE CREAM

Preparation Time: 35 minutes - **Cooking Time:** 0 minutes - **Servings:** 4-6

INGREDIENTS:

- 2 cups heavy cream
- 1 cup milk
- 3/4 cup sugar
- Cannabis butter
- 1 Tbs. vanilla extract
- 1 cup sliced peaches

DIRECTIONS:

1. Using a blender, puree the peaches thoroughly. Place the milk, cream, and cannabis butter in a bowl and mix them together until well combined. Mix in the sugar by using a whisk. Continue to whisk for about 4 minutes until the sugar dissolves. Then mix in the vanilla extract. Then mix in the peaches. Put all the prepared ingredients in a clean ice cream maker and let it churn for 25 minutes. Serve immediately.

Nutrition: Calories: 240, Fat: 6g, Fiber: 2g, Carbs: 56g, Protein: 1.5g

TROPICAL MANGO SOFT SERVE ICE CREAM

Preparation Time: 35 minutes **- Cooking Time:** 0 minutes **- Servings:** 6

INGREDIENTS:

- 2 cups heavy cream
- 1 cup milk
- 3⁄4 cup sugar
- 1 Tbs. vanilla extract
- 1 cup pureed mango (about 2.5 mangos)
- Juice of 1 lime
- Cannabis butter

DIRECTIONS:

1. Puree the mangos with the lime juice in a food processor or blender.
2. Place the milk, cream, and cannabis butter in a bowl and mix them together until well combined. Use a whisk to mix in the sugar. Continue to whisk for about 4 minutes until the sugar dissolves. Then mix in the vanilla extract. Then mix in the mango puree.
3. Put all the prepared ingredients in a clean ice cream maker and let it churn for 25 minutes.
4. Serve immediately.

Nutrition: Calories: 176, Fat: 2.1g, Fiber: 6g, Carbs: 36g, Protein: 0.4g

LIME COCONUT ICE POPS

Preparation Time: 10 minutes **- Cooking Time:** 0 minutes **- Servings:** 4

INGREDIENTS:

- 1 14 ounces canna coconut milk, canned
- 1 cup cream
- 2 tablespoons limeade concentrate
- 1 tablespoon lime zest
- 2 tablespoons lemon juice
- Pinch of salt

DIRECTIONS:

1. Toss in all the ingredients in the blender. Puree until it forms a smooth mix. Transfer mix into Popsicle molds. Freeze molds.

Nutrition: Calories: 180, Fat: 2.5g, Fiber: 8g, Carbs: 35.9g, Protein: 0.2g

ROSE COCONUT ICE CREAM

INGREDIENTS:

- ⅓ cup Rose Tea
- 2 ¾ cup canna cream
- 10 egg yolks
- 5 tablespoons Simple Syrup
- 1 cup coconut, shredded

DIRECTIONS:

1. In a double boiler heat until nearly boiling and remove from the heat rose tea and cream. In a separate bowl, whisk until frothy eggs and milk. Pour the warm milk over the eggs whisking continually, then back into the pan over low heat. Cook and stir until the mixture thickens.
2. The mixture must be strained to a clean bowl and add coconut. Cover with plastic wrap and cool at room temperature. Pour into an electric ice cream machine and follow the manufactures direction.

Nutrition: Calories: 190, Fat: 3.2, Fiber: 3g, Carbs: 45g, Protein: 0.6g

CHAI GREEN TEA ICE CREAM

Preparation Time: 15 minutes - **Cooking Time:** 10-15 minutes - **Servings:** 4-6

INGREDIENTS:

- 2 cups heavy cream
- 2 Chai Tea Blend, dry
- 6 egg yolks
- 1 cup of the warm cream
- ¼ cup instant coffee granular
- 3 tablespoons stevia
- 3 tablespoons canna sugar
- 2 teaspoons vanilla
- ½ cup Chai Tea

DIRECTIONS:

1. Mix everything in under a double boiler and heat up gradually. Once the mixture is smooth and kind of thick, remove from heat and cool down. After this, put in the ice cream maker and churn. Transfer to a container and freeze.

Nutrition: Calories: 199, Fat: 5g, Fiber: 2g, Carbs: 45g, Protein: 0.9g

INDIAN SWEET CARROT PUDDING

Preparation Time: 25 minutes **- Cooking Time:** 30 minutes **- Servings:** 4

INGREDIENTS:

- 5 large carrots shredded
- 1 cup milk
- ½ cup sweetened condensed milk
- ½ cup turbinado sugar
- ½ cup raisins
- ¼ cup raw cashews
- 4 tablespoons Cannabutter
- 1 teaspoon cardamom powder

DIRECTIONS:

1. Place the Cannabutter, raisins and cashews into a frying pan. Sauté this mixture on medium-high for 3 minutes while constantly stirring. Immediately reduce the heat to medium and add in the shredded carrots. Add in the milk, condensed milk and simmer this mixture on medium for 10 minutes while occasionally stirring to break up any clumps. After 10 minutes of simmering, stir in the sugar and continue to cook this mixture in the same setting until the liquid is absorbed by the carrots. This process of allowing the carrots to absorb the liquid will take approximately 15 minutes. Make sure you stir the mixture while it cooks to prevent the mixture from over caramelizing. After the liquid is absorbed, pull from heat and stir in the cardamom powder. Serve this dessert warm from the pan with vanilla ice cream on top or serve it chilled by itself. The plate then serves it by pouring the mixture into a small bowl or large ramekin and allowing it to cool and set to that shape, then turning it out onto a plate. Indian Kalichakra Sweet Carrot Pudding can be stored in the refrigerator for up to 1 week.

Nutrition: Calories: 250, Fat: 4g, Fiber: 1.2g, Carbs: 46g, Protein: 1.4g

SPICY CHICKPEAS

Time: 40 minutes plus cooling time **- Serving Size:** 16 ounces of spiced chickpeas **- Prep Time:** 10 minutes **- Cook Time:** 30 minutes

INGREDIENTS:

- 1 16-ounce can chickpeas

- 2 tablespoon cannabis olive oil
- ¼ teaspoon ground cumin
- ¼ teaspoon ground ginger
- ¼ teaspoon paprika (smoked is preferable, but plain will do just fine)
- ¼ teaspoon salt

Equipment:

- Colander or strainer
- Large mixing bowl
- Baking sheet
- Non-stick cooking spray or parchment paper

DIRECTIONS:

1. Before you prepare the chickpeas, set your oven to 375° F so that it can preheat.
2. Drain the chickpeas in a colander or strainer.
3. Using a large mixing bowl, mix together all the ingredients until the chickpeas are well and evenly coated.
4. Spray a baking sheet with non-stick spray or line it with parchment paper to prevent sticking.
5. Spread the coated nuts out on the baking sheet evenly and bake for 30 minutes or until the chickpeas start to crisp.
6. Allow to cool and store in an airtight container.

SAVORY POPCORN

Time: 15 minutes plus cooling time **- Serving Size:** 1 serving **- Prep Time:** 5 minutes **- Cook Time:** 10 minutes

INGREDIENTS:

- 1/4 cup cannabis-infused butter
- 1/2 cup popcorn kernels
- 1/4 cup canola/vegetable oil
- Salt to taste

Equipment:

Large stockpot with a lid

DIRECTIONS:

1. Over medium-high heat, warm oil in a large stockpot.
2. Drop two to three corn kernels in the oil and cover the pot. When the oil is hot enough, the kernels will pop. When the test kernels pop, add the rest of the corn kernels, spreading them evenly across

the bottom of the pot.

3. Cover the pot and let the kernels pop.

4. Shake the pot gently to shift the kernels so that all of them have a chance to pop.

5. Popping should occur in rapid succession. When the popping slows to two or so seconds between pops, it's time to remove the pot from the heat.

6. Drop the cannabis butter into the pot and mix well to evenly coat the popcorn. Sprinkle with salt as desired.

POTATO CHIPS

Time: 25 minutes - **Serving Size**: 2 servings - **Prep Time:** 10 minutes - **Cook Time:** 15 minutes

INGREDIENTS:

- ¼ cup of cannabis cooking oil

- 1 large potato

- 1 tablespoon salt or 1 tablespoon popcorn seasoning of your choice

Equipment:

- Large baking sheet

- Parchment paper

- Vegetable peeler

- Knife

DIRECTIONS:

1. Set your oven temperature to 400° F and let it heat up while you prepare your potato chips.

2. Line the baking sheet with parchment paper to prevent your chips from sticking.

3. Peel the potato and slice it as thinly as possible into chips. Using a vegetable peeler to slice the chips is effective for achieving thin slices that will crisp well in the oven.

4. Spread out the potato chip slices evenly on your lined baking sheet and drizzle them with the cannabis oil infusion. Coat each chip evenly and well.

5. Place the baking sheet in the center of the preheated oven and bake for about 15 minutes or until golden brown and crispy.

6. Remove the baking sheet from the oven, sprinkle your salt or seasoning over them evenly to taste, and allow the potato chips to cool for about 5 minutes.

BUFFALO CHEX MIX

Time: 55 minutes - **Serving Size:** 3 cups of buffalo Chex mix (serving size suggestion: ¾ cup of mix) - **Prep Time:** 10 minutes - **Cook Time:** 45 minutes

INGREDIENTS:

- ¾ cup Rice Chex cereal
- ¾ cup Corn Chex cereal
- ½ cup rye chips
- ¼ cup of peanuts
- ½ cup small cheddar cheese crackers such as Cheez-Its
- ½ cup pretzels
- ¾ tablespoon cannabis butter
- ¼ tablespoon regular butter
- 1 ounce buffalo sauce
- ¼ packet of dry powdered ranch dressing mix

Equipment:

- Large mixing bowl
- Medium saucepan
- Large baking sheet
- Parchment paper (optional)
- Non-stick cooking spray (optional)

DIRECTIONS:

1. Switch your oven on to 250° F and allow it to preheat while you prepare the mix for baking.
2. Spray a large baking sheet with non-stick cooking spray or, alternatively, line it with a piece of parchment paper and set it aside.
3. In a large mixing bowl, toss the peanuts, crackers, pretzels, both types of Chex cereal, and rye chips and set aside.
4. Set a medium saucepan over medium heat and melt the cannabis butter and regular butter together. Once the butters are melted and combined, mix in the buffalo sauce.
5. Pour the butter and buffalo sauce mixture over the dry ingredients in the mixing bowl and toss well to thoroughly and evenly coat the ingredients.
6. Pour the Chex mix onto your prepared baking sheet, spreading it out evenly in a single layer, and sprinkle the dry ranch dressing over the mix.
7. Place the baking sheet in the center of the oven and bake for 45 minutes. Stir the mix every 15 minutes to prevent clumping and ensure an even bake.
8. Once baked, remove the baking sheet from the oven and place on a countertop to cool. Allow to cool completely and store the buffalo Chex mix in an airtight container for up to one week.

BAKED KALE CHIPS

Time: 20 minutes plus cooling time - **Serving Size:** 2 servings of kale chips - **Prep Time:** 10 minutes -
Cook Time: 10 minutes

INGREDIENTS:

- 1/2 bunch of kale
- 1/2 tablespoon of cannabis butter
- Salt to taste or seasoning spices of your choice

Equipment:

- Baking sheet
- Parchment paper
- Heat-proof ramekin

DIRECTIONS:

1. Preheat your oven by setting the temperature to 375° F and ensure that the oven rack is placed in the center.
2. Line the baking sheet with a piece of parchment paper and set it aside.
3. Wash and thoroughly dry the kale leaves. Remove the stalk from each leaf and then tear each leaf into pieces. The leaf pieces should be around twice the size of a regular tortilla chip. Don't worry if this seems like it's a bit big, the kale chips will shrink in size as they bake so you want to make the raw chips bigger than you want the final baked chips to be.
4. Place the kale chips on the lined baking tray, spreading them out as evenly as possible and ensuring that they form only one layer with no overlapping.
5. Melt the cannabis butter in the ramekin using a microwave. This will only take a few seconds. Alternatively, you can place the ramekin in the preheating oven to melt the butter.
6. Drizzle the melted cannabutter over your spread-out kale leaves. If the coverage isn't sufficient, add some extra regular butter or some olive oil.
7. To ensure even coverage and a better finished kale chip, massage the drizzled butter into each piece of kale leaf. However, you can skip this step if it seems like too much work.
8. Sprinkle the kale with salt or seasoning spices of your choice.
9. Place the baking sheet into the oven and bake the kale for roughly 8 to 10 minutes or until the chips are browned but have not burned.
10. Once baked, remove the baking sheet from the oven and set aside on a countertop to cool off. The kale chips will become crispier as they cool.
11. Store any leftover kale chips in a single layer and cover loosely. Contrary to storage instructions for many other snack foods, don't store your leftovers in an airtight container, as this will cause them

to lose their crisp.

HUSH PUPPIES

Time: 45 minutes - **Serving Size:** Dependent on the size of batter dollops - **Prep Time:** 15 minutes -
Cook Time: 30 minutes

INGREDIENTS:

- 6 cups of your preferred regular cooking oil
- 1 cup of cannabis milk
- 1 ½ cups of self-rising cornmeal
- ½ teaspoon salt
- ½ cup self-rising flour, all-purpose
- ½ teaspoon baking soda
- 1 beaten egg

Equipment:

- Deep fryer
- Mixing bowls
- Teaspoon

DIRECTIONS:

1. Switch the deep fryer on and add the cooking oil, allowing it to heat up to 350° F.
2. Combine the dry ingredients in a mixing bowl and mix well.
3. Using a second mixing bowl, combine the cannabis milk and egg, mixing until incorporated.
4. Add the wet ingredients to the bowl with the dry ingredients and mix thoroughly.
5. Use a teaspoon to scoop out batter and drop it into the hot oil in small dollops. Fry the dollops of batter, turning once, until each side is a rich golden brown color.
6. Be careful not to overcrowd the fryer or to burn the hush puppies. Frying smaller batches at a time offers you better control over the cooking process.
7. Fry all of the batter until finished.
8. Remove each batch of fried hush puppies and lay them between two layers of paper town to absorb any excess oil.
9. Serve warm and enjoy.

HOT CANNA COCOA

Time: 25 minutes - **Serving Size:** 4 servings - **Prep Time:** 5 minutes - **Cook Time:** 20 minutes

INGREDIENTS:

- 6 ounces water
- 3 cups whole milk
- 3 tablespoons unsweetened cocoa powder
- 6 ounces finely chopped semi-sweet chocolate or semi-sweet chocolate chips
- 3 tablespoons sugar
- 1 teaspoon cannabis butter or a few drops of cannabis tincture

Equipment:

- Saucepan
- Whisk
- Mugs

DIRECTIONS:

1. Place the saucepan with the water in it over medium-high heat and let it come to a simmer.
2. Add the cocoa powder and whisk until smooth without lumps.
3. Whisk in the milk and bring the mixture back up to a simmer but not a boil.
4. Add in the sugar and chocolate and continue to whisk for a further five minutes, until the chocolate is completely melted and the whole mixture is creamy and smooth.
5. Pour the hot cocoa into the mugs and stir a teaspoon of cannabis butter into each mug. Alternatively, you can skip the butter and opt to add a few drops of cannabis tincture to your cocoa instead.

LEMONADE

Time: 1 hour 30 minutes **- Serving Size: 8 servings - Prep Time:** 3o minutes **- Cook Time: 1 hour**

INGREDIENTS:

- ½ cup of freshly squeezed lemon juice
- 3 ¼ cups water
- ¼ cup cranberry juice cocktail
- ⅔ cups of sugar
- 4 tablespoons cannabis tincture (Start with half the tincture to test the potency. You can add more as desired.)

Equipment:

- Saucepan
- Large airtight container

DIRECTIONS:

1. Place the saucepan with one cup of water in it over medium-high heat, then add the sugar to the

saucepan. Dissolve the sugar by stirring and bring the mix up to a boil.

2. Once sugar is dissolved, allow the syrup to cool on a counter until it reaches room temperature. Transfer to an airtight container and refrigerate until chilled.

3. Combine the syrup and all the other ingredients in a large pitcher and serve your pink cannabis-infused lemonade chilled over ice cubes.

MARIJUANA MILKSHAKE

Time: 10 minutes **- Serving Size:** 1 serving **- Prep Time:** 5 minutes **- Cook Time:** 5 minutes

INGREDIENTS:

- 2 teaspoons cannabis tincture (Start with half the tincture or only a few drops and increase the dose as desired.)
- 1 cup fresh or frozen strawberries
- 1 teaspoon vanilla extract
- 3/4 cup milk
- 1 cup strawberry ice cream

Equipment:

- Blender

DIRECTIONS:

1. Place all the ingredients into the blender and blend well until incorporated and the milkshake has a smooth consistency.

2. Pour into a mug or glass of your choice and enjoy.

THAI ICED TEA

Time: 15 minutes **- Serving Size:** 6 servings **- Prep Time:** 5 minutes **- Cook Time:** 10 minutes

INGREDIENTS:

- 6 chai tea bags (If you don't have chai tea, you can substitute 6 black tea bags and add in ½ teaspoon of ground cinnamon, one star anise pod, two cardamom pods, and ½ teaspoon vanilla extract.)
- 8 cups boiling water
- 1 14-ounce can condensed milk
- 3 to 5 tablespoons melted cannabis butter
- Optional: ¼ to ½ cup granulated sugar

Equipment:

- Large pitcher

- Small mixing bowl
- 6 glasses

DIRECTIONS:

1. Place your tea bags and spices in a large pitcher and pour in the boiling water. Allow the tea to steep for approximately four to five minutes before removing the tea bags and any whole spices.
2. Set the tea aside and allow it to cool down to room temperature.
3. While the tea is cooling, mix together the cannabutter and the condensed milk and set aside.
4. To serve, fill the six glasses with ice cubes, or half-fill them with crushed ice. Pour the tea into each glass, filling only two-thirds of a glass. Top it all off with two ounces of the condensed milk mixture. The condensed milk mix will sink to the bottom. Stir it all up and enjoy it.

THE PROPER PINEAPPLE SMOOTHIE

Time: 10 minutes **- Serving Size:** 2 servings **- Prep Time:** 5 minutes **- Cook Time:** 5 minutes

INGREDIENTS:

- 2 tablespoons cannabis-infused coconut oil
- 1 cup frozen sliced pineapple
- ¼ cup sliced banana
- ½ cup water
- ½ cup milk
- 1 teaspoon chia seeds (optional)

Equipment:

- Blender

DIRECTIONS:

1. Pack the banana and pineapple into the blender and pour in the water and milk. Blend the lot together until you have achieved a smooth consistency.
2. Gradually and slowly add the two tablespoons of canna coconut oil and blend until well incorporated.
3. Serve the pineapple smoothie in two glasses and top with chia seeds if you'd like.

MAYONNAISE

Time: 2 hours 10 minutes **- Serving Size:** 2 cups of canna mayo **- Prep Time:** 10 minutes **- Cook Time: 2 hours**

INGREDIENTS:

- 3 egg yolks

- 1 cup cannabis oil
- ½ teaspoon Dijon mustard
- 1 teaspoon white vinegar
- 1 teaspoon fresh lemon juice
- A pinch of sea salt

Equipment:

- 1 medium-sized bowl
- Whisk
- 1 appropriately-sized canning jar with a lid

DIRECTIONS:

1. In a medium-sized bowl, whisk together all of the ingredients, except the cannabis oil, until they are well incorporated.
2. Keep whisking and gradually pour the cannaoil into the mixture.
3. Whisk the lot until the mayonnaise starts to get thicker. If it becomes too thick, you can add a few drops of water which will thin it out to your ideal consistency.
4. Pour the canna mayo into the canning jar and allow it to cool to room temperature before sealing and storing it in the fridge.

CAESAR SALAD DRESSING

Time: 20 minutes - **Serving Size:** 2 cups of salad dressing - **Prep Time:** 10 minutes - **Cook Time:** 10 minutes

INGREDIENTS:

- 1 ½ cups cannabis oil
- 2 eggs
- 10 cloves of garlic
- ½ cup lemon juice
- 2 teaspoons sea salt

Equipment:

- A small saucepan
- 1 canning jar with a lid

DIRECTIONS:

1. Pour the water into the saucepan and bring to a boil over medium to high heat.
2. Place the eggs in the water and boil them for 30 seconds. This pasteurizes the eggs.
3. Crack the eggs and combine in a blender with all the other ingredients except the cannaoil. Blend the

concoction for approximately one minute.

4. Keep the blender switched on while slowly adding the cannabis oil to the mixture until everything is well blended.

5. Pour the salad dressing into the jar, seal, and store in the fridge.

6. Give the jar a good shake before serving to mix any ingredients that may have sunken to the bottom of the jar.

LEMON VINAIGRETTE

Time: 15 minutes - **Serving Size:** Approximately 1 ¼ cups of vinaigrette - **Prep Time:** 10 minutes - **Cook Time:** 5 minutes

INGREDIENTS:

- ¼ cup cannabis olive oil
- ¾ cup extra-virgin olive oil
- ¼ cup fresh lemon juice
- ¼ teaspoon honey
- 1 teaspoon minced garlic
- 1 teaspoon dried oregano

Equipment:

- Blender
- 1 bottle or canning jar with a lid

DIRECTIONS:

1. Throw all of the ingredients to your blender, switch it on, and blend until everything is well incorporated. That's it – super simple and easy-to-make vinaigrette.

2. Pour the cannabis-infused vinaigrette into a bottle or jar and store it in the fridge.

3. Give the vinaigrette a good shake before use to mix up any ingredients that may have sunken to the bottom.

BBQ SAUCE

Time: 3 hours 10 minutes - **Serving Size**: 2 cups of sauce - **Prep Time:** 10 minutes - **Cook Time: 3 hours**

INGREDIENTS:

- ⅓ ounce of average decarboxylated cannabis
- ⅓ cup vegetable oil

- Juice of 1 lime
- 2 tablespoons Worcestershire sauce
- 2 tablespoons apple cider vinegar
- 1 tablespoons soy sauce
- ¾ tomato paste
- 1 tablespoon honey
- ½ cup apricot nectar
- ¼ cup water
- 2 tablespoons dark brown sugar
- 1 tablespoon fresh minced garlic
- 3 tablespoons of chopped green onion
- ½ tablespoons chili powder
- A pinch of cayenne pepper
- A pinch of ground ginger

Equipment:

- A crockpot
- 1 canning jar with a lid

DIRECTIONS:

1. Finely crumble the cannabis and put it in a crockpot, along with the water and lime juice. Cook for around two hours.
2. Add the rest of the ingredients to the crockpot and mix well until everything is incorporated.
3. Cook for an additional hour, stirring regularly.
4. Pour your cannabis BBQ sauce into the canning jar and allow it to cool to room temperature before sealing. Store your sauce in the fridge and give it a shake before use so that any ingredients that sink to the bottom get mixed up again.

PESTO

Time: 15 minutes - **Serving Size:** Approximately 1 cup of pesto - **Prep Time:** 10 minutes - **Cook Time:** 5 minutes

INGREDIENTS:

- Walnuts
- ¼ cup freshly grated Parmesan cheese
- 1 cup cannabis-infused olive oil
- 2 cloves garlic

- 2 cups basil
- A pinch of sea salt

Equipment:

- 1 canning jar with a lid
- Blender
- Saucepan

DIRECTIONS:

1. Use medium heat to warm up a skillet and toast the pine nuts. This will take approximately three minutes. Keep stirring the nuts to prevent them from burning.
2. Take the saucepan off the heat and let the pine nuts cool down.
3. Put the pine nuts in your blender and blend on high until they are ground up to resemble a coarse flour.
4. Rinse the basil off and pat dry with a paper towel before removing the stems and breaking the leaves into small pieces.
5. Add all of the remaining ingredients except the cannaoil to the ground pine nuts in the blender.
6. Switch the processor on medium to low speed and, while it's blending the ingredients, gradually add 1/3 of the cup of cannaoil. Add the basil, garlic, salt, and Parmesan to the walnut flour in the food processor.
7. Taste the pesto and add more salt or cannaoil until the taste and consistency is to your liking.

SRIRACHA HOT SAUCE

Time: 24 hours - **Serving Size:** Approximately 1 cup of sriracha sauce - **Prep Time**: 10 minutes - **Cook Time: 24 hours**

INGREDIENTS:

- ½ cup cannabis cooking oil
- 8 cloves of garlic
- 12 hot chili peppers of your choice (The hotter the peppers, the hotter your siracha will be.)
- ¼ cup apple cider vinegar
- 3 tablespoons of honey (You can use cannabis-infused honey for an extra kick if you like.)

Equipment:

- Aluminum foil
- A baking sheet
- A blender/food processor
- 1 canning jar with a lid

DIRECTIONS:

1. Switch your oven on and preheat it to 350° F.
2. Cover the baking sheet with aluminum foil so that every inch of it is covered.
3. Lay the chili peppers on the foil-covered sheet and roast them for 10 minutes.
4. Remove the sheet from the oven and rotate the peppers.
5. Spread the garlic evenly on the baking sheet and return it to the oven to bake for a further 10 minutes.
6. Remove the baking sheet from the oven and allow the peppers and garlic to cool until you can handle them without burning your fingers. Remove the stems from the chili peppers.
7. Put the peppers and garlic into the food processor along with the rest of the ingredients. You can also always add some more garlic if you like a lot of garlic.
8. Turn that blender on and keep going until everything is blended together and your sriracha sauce has a smooth consistency. If you like it a bit chunkier, simply blend until the sauce reaches your desired chunkiness.
9. Pour the sauce into the canning jar and allow it to cool completely.
10. Seal the jar and store in the fridge. Allow your sriracha sauce to sit for 24 hours before you use it so that all the flavors meld together.

NACHO CHEESE SAUCE

Time: 25 minutes - **Serving Size:** Serves 6 - **Prep Time:** 5 minutes - **Cook Time:** 20 minutes

INGREDIENTS:

- 2 tablespoons cannabis butter
- 1 cup whole milk at room temperature
- 2 tablespoons flour
- 1 ½ cup shredded/grated cheddar cheese
- ¼ teaspoon salt (or to taste)
- ¼ teaspoon pepper (or to taste)
- Optional extras: a pinch of cayenne/cumin/garlic powder

Equipment:

- A skillet
- Whisk

DIRECTIONS:

1. Use medium heat to get the skillet warmed up and melt the cannabis-infused butter.
2. Add in the flour and whisk well. The mixture should become crumb-like or even form a paste.
3. Slowly and gradually add the milk while whisking like crazy to smooth out the mixture and break up

any lumps. Keep whisking away as the mixture reaches a simmer.

4. Sprinkle in cheddar cheese a bit at a time. Don't add too much at once, and spread it out to avoid cheese lumps.
5. Keep whisking – nacho cheese dip requires a lot of whisking and a good whisking arm. As you add cheese to the dipping sauce, allow the previous lot to melt completely before adding more.
6. Add the seasonings that you prefer to use for this dip.
7. Enjoy the cheesy goodness immediately – do not refrigerate and reheat it, as this spoils the texture.

PEANUT BUTTER

Time: 10 minutes **- Serving Size:** 1 serving **- Prep Time:** 5 minutes **- Cook Time:** 5 minutes

INGREDIENTS:

- 2 tablespoons peanut butter of your choice
- 2 teaspoons cannabis infused cooking oil

Equipment:

- Spoon
- Bowl

DIRECTIONS:

1. Combine the cannabis oil infusion and the peanut butter in a small bowl and stir well until thoroughly incorporated.
2. If the consistency is not thick enough, chill in the fridge for a short while to stiffen the peanut butter up.

HUMMUS

Time: 10 minutes **- Serving Size:** 1 cup of hummus **- Prep Time:** 5 minutes **- Cook Time:** 5 minutes

INGREDIENTS:

- 7.5 ounces of cooked chickpeas (also called garbanzo beans)
- 1/8 cup tahini
- 1/8 cup of freshly squeezed lemon juice, strained
- 2 cloves of garlic, fresh
- ½ an ounce to 1 ounce of cannabis-infused cooking oil such as canola or olive oil (the amount you add will depend on how potent you want the hummus to be)
- ¼ teaspoon cumin, ground
- 1 to 2 tablespoons of water

- Salt and pepper to taste

Equipment:

- Blender or food processor
- Bowl

DIRECTIONS:

1. Using a blender or a food processor, mix the tahini and the lemon juice together and blend for about 30 seconds.
2. Add in all of the remaining ingredients but only half of the water and blend the lot together well until you have a smooth texture. This will take approximately one minute.
3. If the hummus is too stiff or thick, add a little bit more water and blend again until you reach the consistency you want.
4. Pour the hummus from the blender or processor into a serving or dipping bowl and enjoy.

GUMMY SWEETS

Time: 45 minutes - **Serving Size:** 12 servings - **Prep Time:** 5 minutes - **Cook Time:** 40 minutes

INGREDIENTS:

- 2 tablespoons unflavored plain gelatin
- 1 3-ounce package of flavored Jell-O
- ½ cup canna coconut oil
- ½ cup of cold water
- ½ teaspoon of soy or sunflower lecithin (optional)

Equipment:

- Whisk
- Cooking pot
- Ladle or dropper
- Gummy bear mold or another food-safe mold of your choice

DIRECTIONS:

1. Put a pot over low heat and add the water, canna coconut oil, and the lecithin if you're using it.
2. Allow the mixture to heat up, stirring constantly, until the oil has melted.
3. Stir in the unflavored and flavored gelatins.
4. Continue whisking the mixture for about 10 to 15 minutes until the gelatin has been entirely dissolved and incorporated. Keep the heat low and do not allow the mixture to reach a boil.
5. Once the 15 minutes is up, use a dropper or a ladle to fill the molds. It is crucial to work quickly while filling the molds, as the mixture could start to cool and separate.

6. Keep whisking the mixture in the pot between pouring to keep the mixture well combined.

7. When a mold is filled, lift it off the countertop slightly and drop it to dislodge any air bubbles in your gummy mixture.

8. Transfer the molds to the freezer for approximately 25 minutes.

Tip: Toss the ganja gummies in cornstarch to prevent them from sticking together after removing them from the molds.

CANNABIS CHOCOLATE

Time: 25 minutes plus cooling time **- Serving Size:** Makes enough chocolate for 2 people **- Prep Time:** 10 minutes **- Cook Time:** 15 minutes

INGREDIENTS:

- ⅛ cup cannabis-infused butter
- 1 cups chocolate
- Pieces of dried fruit or nuts (optional)

Equipment:

- Pot
- Glass bowl that fits onto the pot to create a makeshift double-boiler
- Chocolate bar molds or other food-safe molds
- Ladle

DIRECTIONS:

1. Fill the pot halfway with water and bring to a gentle simmer over medium heat.

2. Put the chocolate into the glass bowl and place the bowl into the top of the pot so that the bottom is not touching the simmering water.

3. Put your cannabutter into the bowl with the chocolate and allow everything to melt completely, stirring to combine.

4. Ladle or pour the melted chocolate into the molds and rap the molds on the countertop to dislodge any air bubbles.

5. If you are adding fruit or nuts to your chocolate, do so now and press the pieces into the chocolate slightly.

6. Refrigerate your canna chocolate immediately until it is set and firm.

CHOCOLATE CHIP CANNA COOKIES

Time: 25 minutes **- Serving Size:** Dependent on the size of the cookies **- Prep Time:** 15 minutes **- Cook Time:** 10 minutes

INGREDIENTS:

- 2 cups and 1/3 heaped cup all-purpose flour
- 3/4 cup granulated white sugar
- 1 cup granulated brown sugar
- 1 ounce regular butter
- 6 ounces cannabis-infused butter
- 2 large eggs
- 1 teaspoon baking soda
- 1 teaspoon salt
- 1 teaspoon vanilla extract
- 1 3/4 cups chocolate chips

Equipment:

- Baking sheets
- Non-stick cooking spray
- Large mixing bowl
- Large mixing spoon

DIRECTIONS:

1. Spray your baking sheets with the non-stick spray and set them aside.
2. Turn your oven to 375° F and let it preheat while mixing the cookie dough.
3. In a small bowl, mix together the baking soda, flour, and salt.
4. In a large bowl, cream the regular and cannabis butter, sugars, and vanilla extract.
5. One at a time, add the eggs to the butter mixture and combine well.
6. Slowly add the flour mix to the butter mixture, stirring in one cup at a time.
7. Pour in the chocolate chips and stir to distribute them evenly throughout the dough.
8. Roll the dough into balls, arrange them on the baking sheets and flatten slightly.
9. Bake the cookies for between 9 and 11 minutes or until done.

MALLOW BARS

Time: 30 minutes plus cooling time - **Serving Size:** Dependent on the size of the mallow bars when cut - **Prep Time:** 10 minutes - **Cook Time:** 20 minutes

INGREDIENTS:

- 1 pack of marshmallows
- ¼ cup of cannabis butter
- 6 cups of Cinnamon Toast Crunch cereal, Rice Krispies, or Fruit Loops

Equipment:

- 13" x 9" x 2" pan
- Non-stick cooking spray or butter for greasing
- Large saucepan or pot

DIRECTIONS:

1. Evenly coat the pan in non-stick spray or butter, making sure to get into the corners.
2. Using low heat, put the cannabutter in the saucepan and melt it. Stir to prevent burning.
3. Empty the entire bag of marshmallows into the saucepan. Stir the marshmallows and melted butter until all the marshmallows are fully melted.
4. Remove the saucepan from the heat and add in the cereal of your choice. Mix the whole lot together to evenly coat the cereal with the marshmallow mix.
5. Pour the mixture into the prepared pan, ensuring that it is evenly spread across the pan.
6. Press down firmly to compact the mixture so that it will hold its shape once set.
7. Allow the bars to cool at room temperature or pop them in the fridge to speed up the process. If you refrigerate them, allow them to warm up a little before slicing.
8. Slice the cereal bars into blocks according to your size preference.

CHOCOLATE CANNA CLUSTERS

Time: 40 minutes plus cooling time **- Serving Size:** Dependent on the size of the clusters **- Prep Time:** 10 minutes **- Cook Time:** 30 minutes

INGREDIENTS:

- 6 ounces of semi-sweet chocolate chips
- 1 1/2 cups chopped pecans
- 1/2 cup cannabis-infused butter
- 1 pinch salt
- 2/3 cup sweetened condensed milk
- 1 cup firmly packed light brown sugar
- 1/2 cup light corn syrup
- 1/2 teaspoon vanilla extract

Equipment:

- 2 baking sheets
- Non-stick cooking spray
- Saucepan
- Candy or cooking thermometer

DIRECTIONS:

1. Grease the baking trays and arrange the chopped pecans in little clusters on the sheets. Spread them out evenly and set them aside.
2. Over medium heat, melt the cannabis butter in a saucepan. Once melted, stir in the sugar and salt until the sugar dissolves.
3. Add in the sweetened condensed milk and corn syrup and allow it to cook until the concoction reaches a temperature of 250° F. Use the thermometer to check the temperature of the mixture. Stir the mixture regularly to prevent burning. This should take around 15 to 20 minutes.
4. Add the vanilla extract and then place spoonfuls of the caramel mixture on top of the pecan clusters. Set the trays aside for the caramel to cool and harden.
5. Over medium-low to low heat, melt the chocolate chips carefully in a saucepan until the melted chocolate is smooth. Stir constantly to prevent burning.
6. Once the caramels have cooled and firmed up, you can either dip them in the chocolate, generously drizzle the chocolate over them, or spoon blobs of chocolate on top of them.
7. Set aside to cool completely and set the chocolate.

GRANOLA BARS

Time: 25 minutes plus cooling time - **Serving Size:** 16 bars - **Prep Time:** 10 minutes - **Cook Time:** 15 minutes

INGREDIENTS:

- 2 1/2 cups old-fashioned rolled oats
- 1/2 cup roughly chopped nuts (almonds, pecans, cashews)
- 1/4 cup honey
- 2 tablespoons cannabis-infused butter
- 2 tablespoons unsalted butter
- 1/3 cup brown sugar
- 1 teaspoon vanilla extract
- 3/4 cups additional ingredients of your choice

Options include:

- Sunflower seeds
- Shredded coconut
- Dried blueberries
- Dried cranberries
- Dried cherries

- Dried pineapple
- Dried mandarin oranges
- Dried mango
- Chopped-up pretzels
- Chocolate chips (dark chocolate, milk chocolate, semi-sweet, white chocolate)
- Peanut butter chips
- M&Ms
- Peanut butter M&Ms
- Chopped peppermint candy
- Reese's Pieces
- 1/4 cup peanut butter (If using peanut butter, only use ½ a cup of other add-ins.)

Equipment:

- 9" baking pan
- Non-stick cooking spray or parchment paper
- Large bowl
- Small saucepan

DIRECTIONS:

1. Spray the pan with non-stick spray or line it with parchment paper to prevent sticking.
2. In a large bowl, mix the nuts and the oats.
3. Using medium heat, melt and mix together the honey, brown sugar, cannabis butter, and regular butter until the sugar has fully dissolved and everything is well combined. Stir regularly to prevent burning.
4. Remove from the heat and add in the salt and vanilla extract. If you are choosing to use ¼ cup of peanut butter, add this now. Stir everything together until well combined.
5. Pour this mixture over the nuts and oats in the bowl. Throw your add-ins into the bowl, as well except for any form of chocolate or chocolate-coated candy if you are using any.
6. Mix it all up until everything is well coated.
7. Let the mixture cool and then add chocolate if you are using any.
8. Pour the granola bar mix into the baking pan, spreading it evenly and pressing down firmly to compact the mixture for firmer bars that are less likely to fall apart.
9. Pop the pan into the fridge for a minimum of two hours or up to overnight.
10. Slice the granola into 16 bars, remove from the pan, and enjoy.
11. Store your ganja granola bars in the freezer.

Tips: Lay the nuts and oats on a baking sheet, evenly spread out, and bake them for around eight or so minutes to lightly toast them. Toasting the oats and nuts will lend a cookie-like flavor to your granola bars. Crumble the granola bars over yogurt or into milk for a quick and tasty breakfast option.

BLUEBERRY MUFFINS

Time: 35 minutes plus cooling time - **Serving Size:** 6 muffins - **Prep Time:** 10 minutes - **Cook Time:** 25 minutes

INGREDIENTS:

- ½ cup frozen or fresh blueberries
- 1 cup all-purpose flour
- 1 teaspoon baking powder
- ⅛ teaspoon salt
- ½ teaspoon vanilla extract
- 1 egg
- ½ cup of sugar
- ¼ cup milk
- ⅛ cup unsalted butter
- ¾ cup cannabis-infused butter

Equipment:

- Large mixing bowl
- Muffin pan
- Non-stick baking spray
- Cooling rack

DIRECTIONS:

2. Set your oven to 375° F and let it preheat while you make the muffin batter.
3. Spray the cups of your muffin pan with non-stick spray and set it aside.
4. In a large mixing bowl, combine the baking powder, salt, and flour and mix well.
5. Create a well in the center of the flour mixture and cut the cannabis butter up into blocks, dropping them into the well. Use your fingers to rub the butter into the flour to form crumbs.
6. Add the sugar and mix well.
7. Crack the eggs into the mixture and beat until you achieve a creamy texture.
8. Slowly add the milk and vanilla extract and mix well until combined. Do not over-mix.
9. Fold the blueberries gently into the batter until evenly distributed throughout.
10. Spoon or ladle the batter into the cups of the muffin pan, filling a maximum of 2/3 of each cup. Start by filling ½ of each cup until all cups are half-filled. Afterward, go back and add to each cup until all 12 cups are evenly filled with batter.

11. Pop the muffin pan into the oven and bake for 20 to 25 minutes, or until the muffins have risen and an inserted toothpick comes out clean.

12. Remove from the oven when done, turn out onto a cooling rack, and allow the muffins to cool.

13. Store in the fridge in a Ziploc bag for a grab-and-go-breakfast or snack or keep in the freezer for a later date.

SALTED CARAMEL POPCORN

Time: 25 minutes **- Serving Size:** 2 servings of 3 cups each **- Prep Time:** 10 minutes **- Cook Time:** 15 minutes

INGREDIENTS:

- 6 cups of popped popcorn, plain
- ½ ounce of cannabutter
- 1/8 cup regular butter
- ½ cup dark brown sugar
- 1/8 cup honey
- 1 teaspoon sea salt (regular table salt will also do the trick)
- 1/3 teaspoon baking soda
- ½ teaspoon of either vanilla or maple extract

Equipment:

- 2 large baking sheets
- Parchment paper (optional)
- Medium-sized saucepan
- Candy thermometer (optional)
- Large bowl

DIRECTIONS:

1. Switch on your oven to 225° F and let it preheat while you prep your popcorn.

2. Pop your popcorn using an air fryer, a regular popcorn maker, a microwave, or a pot on the stovetop. Once you have popped your corn, set it aside in a large bowl.

3. Grease or line your baking sheets. You can use parchment paper to line them or you can grease them with butter. Be sure to use a generous amount of butter if you are choosing to grease the trays. Set the lined or greased trays aside.

4. Set your stovetop to medium heat and melt the cannabis butter in the saucepan.

5. Once the cannabutter is melted, add the brown sugar, honey, and ¼ teaspoon of the salt. Stir until all the ingredients are dissolved and then continue to cook the mixture until it reaches a boil, stirring

regularly.

6. When the mixture comes to a boil, reduce the heat to a simmer. If you have a candy thermometer handy, you can use this to tell when the caramel mix reaches a temperature of 250° F. If you don't have a candy thermometer, don't fret — you can get quite close to the right temperature by letting the mixture cook at a simmer for about 1 ½ minutes.

7. When the caramel mixture is ready, remove the saucepan from the heat and stir in the baking soda and your choice of extract. Add these ingredients quickly and stir, the mixture will turn a light brown color and become frothy.

8. It is important to work quickly at this point in the cooking process because the caramel will start to cool and harden.

9. Quickly pour the caramel over the popcorn you set aside earlier. Toss the popcorn in the caramel or stir the mixture through thoroughly until the popcorn is completely and evenly coated.

10. Spread your coated popcorn out on the baking sheets. Ensure that each baking sheet only has a single layer of evenly spread popcorn.

11. Sprinkle the coated popcorn with the remaining salt.

12. Place the baking sheets into the oven and bake the popcorn for 15 minutes.

13. After 15 minutes, remove the baking sheets from the oven and break the popcorn mixture up into pieces by giving it a good stir.

14. Place the baking sheets back in the oven and let the mix bake for a further 15 minutes.

15. Once done, remove the baking sheets from the oven and allow your salted caramel popcorn to cool. To store the balance, place it in an airtight container once it has completely cooled down.